reclaiming our stories

reclaiming our stories

narratives of identity, resilience and empowerment

edited by:

Mona Alsoraimi-Espiritu
Roberta Alexander
Manuel Paul López

SD
CWP

SAN DIEGO
CITY WORKS
PRESS

ISBN 978-0-9765801-5-7
Library of Congress Control Number: 2016943977

San Diego City Works Press is a non-profit press, funded by local writers and friends of the arts, committed to the publication of fiction, poetry, creative nonfiction, and art by members of the San Diego City College community and the community at large. For more about San Diego City Works Press please visit our website at www.cityworkspress.org.

San Diego City Works Press is extremely indebted to the American Federation of Teachers, Local 1931, without whose generous contribution and commitment to the arts this book would not be possible.

Cover design: Rondi Vasquez
Cover photo: Sarah Loud
Production editor: Will Dalrymple | Layout & Editing | http://www.willdalrymple.com

Published in the United States by San Diego City Works Press, California
Printed in the United States of America

table of contents

additional resources

foreword

Reclaiming Our Stories: A Soul-stirring Achievement

Elbert "Big Man" Howard

Several weeks ago, I received a manuscript from my friend, Professor Roberta Alexander. She asked me to write a few lines about the content and told me it was awaiting publication. This seemed like a simple request and so I agreed and proceeded to leaf through the material. I soon realized, as I proceeded to give time and thought to each story, that I was captured by the words of each and every one of them and surprised by the emotions they stirred within me.

For me, reading this group of autobiographical narratives was a very rare experience. Each individual story, simply but eloquently told, reached out and pulled me into it and touched me emotionally, deeply and profoundly. Many reached out and pulled me into dark places that are not pleasant for me to visit. Some of these writings brought me to tears but almost all of them had me cheering and marveling with joy because of these writers' ultimate healing and their victories over the dreadful, tragic events in their lives.

In my view, getting a community of writers together, challenging them, giving them the guidance needed and helping to instill the desire and confidence, as well as recognizing the need and the importance of putting their histories into the written word, is a revolutionary concept producing revolutionary results.

This collection is a monumental achievement for all the writers and their mentors and should be shared far and wide. It will lay the inspirational groundwork for exceptional works by so many unheard voices. I salute the Southeast San Diego Pillars of the Community and the writers, along with the mentors/professors for their courage and hard work in producing this project, *Reclaiming Our Stories*. I can hardly wait to see this manuscript out in literary print and watch the world share in my experience.

June 14th, 2016
Santa Rosa, CA

Elbert "Big Man" Howard is one of the original six founding members of the Black Panther Party and the first editor of the Black Panther Party Newspaper. *He is also one of the founding members of the Police Accountability Clinic and Helpline (PACH). An activist, author and lecturer, he resides in Sonoma County.*

acknowledgments

We are grateful to Sarah Loud for contributing her time and expertise in the photos in this text; to Jess Jollett for her support in brainstorming and coordinating; to Will Dalrymple and Rondi Vasquez for their labors of love for helping us realize the design and layout of the interior text, and the cover. We especially want to thank Kelly Mayhew and Jim Miller, managing editors of City Works Press, for having the confidence in our project and its importance, to grant us the opportunity to publish these community stories. We would also like to give a shout out to Paul Alexander for his inspiration for doing a project like Reclaiming Our Stories, and to Mona Alsoraimi-Espiritu for making it happen.

Above all, we appreciate the over ten years of work and dedication as well as financial donations that have gone into the success of City Works Press.

introduction

You are about to read a collection of stories by our neighbors and friends who are dedicating their lives to making positive changes in their communities, and in many cases are pursuing their educational goals. Many are, or have been, students at San Diego City College; some have completed their educational goals at other colleges and universities. Most, if not all, are first generation college students. They have all survived and continue their struggle to overcome the constant challenges of being black, brown and poor in San Diego. These narratives deal with such complex issues as race, class, place, family, gender, and identity. Above all, however, they are stories of life, loss, and determination to thrive.

These stories offer a glimpse into the lives of real people in their own words; they put a human face to members of our communities who have been marginalized, labeled as criminals, and discarded by our society.

The Reclaiming Our Stories project was first launched in the summer of 2015. Initially our writers got together in a shared space at the Southeast San Diego Pillars of the Community office to write about any aspect of their lives—to brainstorm, share, make suggestions, and to support one another. A few of us served as facilitators, but the most important feedback came from the entire community of writers. Our goal was to complete the process by having gatherings where everybody read their stories to family and friends. In the months that we worked together, we built a trusting community of writers, and by finally reading their stories to an audience, most of our writers recognized and expressed that the experience had in many ways been both cathartic and healing.

The intention of the Reclaiming Our Stories project was never to publish the stories. It was to share experiences and build community through common struggles and achievements. When the managing editors of City Works Press offered us the possibility of publishing our narratives, we decided to pursue the opportunity to bring these powerful stories to a broader audience. Once the decision was made to publish, it was with the understanding that everyone would be published. Everyone agreed to accept the opportunity and challenge of preparing stories that were written to be presented orally to an audience into narratives that would be read as texts.

Some of you will recognize these experiences and have lived them; others of you will learn about an aspect of life in our communities that you have not known. Each of our writers has participated in the process in a different way. Some sat down at our first gathering and cranked out their entire story. Others were not ready to face elements of their past, let alone write about them.

The authors of these stories took great risk in sharing their personal narratives. Although it wasn't the intention of the project, most authors chose to write about some of the most traumatic events in their lives. These are often honest reflections of ugly and painful realities that our authors have dealt with, often from a young age—the human stories of the consequences of systemic racism as well as the consequences of a society in which we do not all have equal opportunity to thrive. These are stories of children who have suffered incredible trauma who are not helped; of young people who have drowned their pain through the abuse of alcohol and drugs; of those who grew up in environments where the only role models were gang members and hustlers; of a criminal "justice" system that has—"[m]ore African Americans in prison, jail, on probation or parole [than] were enslaved in 1850, before the Civil War began";[1] of

---

1   See p. 175 in Michelle Alexander's *The New Jim Crow: Mass Incarceration in the Age of Colorblindness*.

the human consequences of legal lynch codes, like the California Penal Code 182.5,[2] that allow people to be arrested, tried and convicted for offenses that everyone, including the district attorney, knows they were not involved in; of homelessness; of immigrant families torn asunder by unfair immigration practices; of broken families; of neighborhoods where gangs and violence are commonplace.

It is our hope that you will gain new insight into the lives of members of our community, as told through their own words.

Mona Alsoraimi-Espiritu
Manuel Paul López
Roberta Alexander
Darius Spearman

---

2   For more information on Penal Code 182.5, please see "Guest Lecture: Guilty by Association? Aaron Harvey and Brandon 'Tiny Doo' Duncan Speak at San Diego City College," *African Elements*, June 12, 2015 at http://africanelements.org/guest-lecture-guilty-by-association-aaron-harvey-and-brandon-tiny-doo-duncan-speak-at-san-diego-city-college/. Additionally, for a list of the nine criteria used by the San Diego Police Department to document gang members and how those criteria are used, please visit "Frequently Asked Questions Regarding Identifying Gangs and Gang Members" at https://www.sandiego.gov/sites/default/files/legacy/gangcommission/pdf/sgufaq.pdf.

the stories

Tariq Ali was born and raised in Bronx, New York to a family that was heavily involved in gangs and drugs. He joined a gang at the age of ten and eventually worked his way up into a leadership position. His involvement in the gang lifestyle led him to being shot multiple times and to facing life in prison. While there, he decided to leave the gang and accept Islam as his new path. After six years he was released from prison and now works in Southeast San Diego with Pillars of the Community in an effort to steer kids away from gangs.

Tariq Ali
Mi Abuelita, My Grandma

To my abuelita, who used to tell me, "El que no coge consejo no llega a viejo." He who doesn't take advice won't reach old age.

I will never forget the day I was shot. It was May 1993. As I lay in the emergency room, my body riddled with bullets, I was sure I was going to die. How could I not have thought that? How many people could get shot eight times and survive? Thank God I was wrong because several hours later I awoke in the hospital after a successful surgery.

When I feel the sensation of water dripping on my face, I open my eyes and I see my grandmother and my auntie, and alongside them a man who I've never seen before and who I eventually find out is a priest. See, I was never baptized as a child and since my family is Catholic, they thought it would be of utmost importance to baptize me just in case I wouldn't make it.

What impacted me most was not the presence of the priest, nor was it the baptism, instead it was the pain I saw in my abuelita's eyes as I lay there on the operating table. It was the way she was hugging and kissing me, telling me how much she loved me, tears rolling down her cheeks as she saw her baby clinging to life.

Although seeing me lying there on that operating table was one of the most painful moments in my grandmother's life, pain and sorrow was nothing new to her. My grandmother died at the age of 88 and I can honestly say that most of those years were spent suffering due to the hell her children put her through, including myself. I grew up in the South Bronx in a family full of gang members and drug users. Both my mother and father were gang members; in fact, it was actually in the gangs where they met. I guess you can call it "Thug Love," except for the fact that there was really no love.

According to all narrations, my mother and father's relationship was a volatile one to say the least. At 22 years of age, my father had just come home from Vietnam and my mother, a young 15-year-old, could not help but be in awe of the military man, a real man as compared to all the young boys in the neighborhood. She immediately fell in love, or at least she thought she was in love with this soldier, this fighter, this warrior, but unfortunately the reality was that my father was nothing but a heroin addict who suffered from a severe case of PTSD or Post Traumatic Stress Disorder, a combination which led to his violent tendencies towards others but were mostly directed at my mother who eventually also became a heroin addict.

This relationship came to an abrupt end when my father took me from my mother—not necessarily because he cared for me or wanted to raise me, but simply because he knew it would hurt her. My mother, being so young and addicted to drugs, didn't fight for me, and since my father couldn't raise me, in came this five-foot three-inch, grey-haired woman with big glasses, my abuelita, my grandmother, my superhero to save the day.

She snatched me away from my father and decided to raise me as her own. Although she did her best to raise me right, I was surrounded by her other children, all of whom were also gang members and drug users. And as they say, we were all products of our own environment. So I never dreamed of being a doctor or a lawyer; instead, I wanted to be a gang member. I always looked at my uncles and even my aunts as some of the hardest gangsters. I wanted so much to be like them, and that desire to follow in their footsteps eventually led me to my current condition, which was a body filled with eight bullets and my dear grandmother crying and praying to Jesus to save her child.

Although looking at the pain in my grandmother's eyes had a powerful impact on me, it was short-lived because my thoughts went from feeling sorrow and regret to anger and revenge. How was I going to get back at them? Who was I going to shoot first?

See, the code of the streets is that when you get hit, it is incumbent upon you to not just hit back, but to hit harder and with more force. As my uncle, Sporty B, once told me, "They take one of yours and you take two of theirs," and although that seems like a quote from the movies, that, in fact, was my reality. I didn't see the people I rolled with as a gang but as a family, and like any family, my love for them was unconditional. This turned out to be one of the biggest mistakes I could have made in my life and only proves in retrospect how brainwashed I had become.

When I was growing up, I only got to see the outward manifestation of what a gang or street organization was. I saw that they all moved as one, with one goal and one purpose. I saw the money, the respect, the girls, the fear that others had of them and the love that they had for one another. That was so attractive to me. I wanted it so bad that I was willing to live and die for it, and I almost did.

Because the outward manifestation of that life was so attractive, so appealing to me, I never stopped to reflect on the inner demons that many of my so-called brothers, my hermanitos, were dealing with. I recently heard a saying that goes something to the effect, "One cannot give what one does not have," so if you never experienced the reality of love then how can you give it to someone else? I, as well as many other kids in what would be considered the ghetto, have grown up chasing that love, wanting that love and acceptance all of our lives, but that desire for love often blinds us to reality.

I was ten years old when I first got jumped into a gang. It was in the schoolyard of CES 90 in the South Bronx. There were three kids a bit older than me. We four got in the center surrounded by about 15 other kids. Jughead, the pres, said: "Are you ready?" I said, "Yeah, I'm ready," and next thing I knew, the three kids started whipping on me. I swung back, feeling the contact of my fists against their faces, but mostly I felt the contact of their fists and feet all throughout my body which only led me to the conclusion that I was on the floor being stomped out mercilessly for what felt like an eternity. Eventually, Jughead screamed, "Time, that's it!" I got up and had about 18 kids hugging and patting me on my back and giving me dap. Jughead finally came up to me and said, "You did it hermanito, we family now." Ah, yes! I finally got what I'd been looking for, that love, that brotherhood, a family. But as I lay up in the hospital ten years later with eight bullets in me, I now wondered, where was that love? What ever happened to that brotherhood? Where was the family that I so desired, that family that I yearned for?

Wait! Can it be? Is it possible that I have been that blind and that brainwashed that I just never realized that what I had been chasing after most of my life was always there? Grandma, my abuelita, I love you too; don't cry, I'm going to be all right. Or at least that's what I thought.

About a month or so later:
ABC, Channel 7 Eyewitness News

> Breaking news: 20 leaders of one of New York City's most notorious criminal gangs, the Latin Kings, were charged yesterday with attempted murder, murder, racketeering, heroin and cocaine trafficking, and other crimes in an 80-count federal indictment.

Damn! Now I am being transferred from Bellevue Hospital's criminal ward to the Metropolitan Correctional Center in New York, a federal jail, facing the rest of my life in prison and all I can think about is not the bullet holes, not even the fact that I may have to spend the rest of my life in prison but instead what's going to happen when this news reaches the woman who has always loved me unconditionally, my strength, my support, my superhero, my abuelita?

Mona Abdul Karim Alsoraimi-Espiritu is an English professor at San Diego City College. Although she has been in San Diego for 15 years, she grew up in Dearborn, a small, primarily Arab suburb of Detroit, Michigan. Her father immigrated to the United States from Yemen as a young man to seek better opportunities and her mother's family fled the violence and oppression in Palestine caused by the Israeli occupation. They relocated to Jordan, and later the United States. Mona served as a Peace Corps volunteer in both Mongolia and Jordan where she worked in education and community development. She continues to work on community development at City College and with Pillars of the Community.

Mona Abdul Karim Alsoraimi-Espiritu
Terrorist?

You cannot continue to victimize someone because you yourself were a victim once—there has to be a limit.

—Edward Said on the Israeli occupation of Palestine

Growing up, I remember hearing my aunt chant, "Reagan, Reagan, don't you know, we support the PLO!"—a popular chant at demonstrations supporting the liberation of Palestine at the time. I grew up seeing and hearing my relatives speak freely about Palestinian politics and never feeling afraid to express their opinions about the oppression that was and still is taking place in Palestine and in other places in the Middle East. We spoke our minds and never hesitated to tell people that we were Palestinian and Yemeni.

I had been living in San Diego for a couple of years when one cool spring night, a few months after 9-11, at the five-star steakhouse where I worked as a hostess, my shift began. Like most Thursday nights, it was moderately busy and I stood outside the restaurant's expansive foyer greeting customers that walked in. A middle-aged, white couple walked up and since they didn't have reservations, I let them know that it would be a 15-minute wait. As they waited, they stood under the high ceilings of the foyer and like many out-of-town and bored customers, began to chat me up. I swallowed my sigh, forced a smile and prepared to make small talk.

One of their first questions, as usual, was about my ethnic background. "Where are you from?" they asked eagerly. And, as usual, I answered with something snarky like, "Detroit," and predictably they followed with, "No really, like where are you really from?" The conversation was off to a great start. Being accustomed to this line of questioning, I didn't suspect anything unusual. When I said "Yemeni," they seemed uninterested, but the "Palestinian" part piqued their interest. This was before al Qaeda and drone attacks in Yemen and after 9-11. Upon hearing the word "Palestinian" loosely escape my lips, their bodies stiffened, while they tightened their grips on their glasses that held top-shelf cocktails. They continued to engage me in conversation involving a series of "innocent" questions about Palestinian politics, and I, at the naive age of 19, participated honestly and openly. They were warm, and seemingly easy-going and friendly and seemed interested in what I had to say. I took their smiles and questions as a sign that they wanted to engage in a real conversation, and that was okay with me. Having grown up in Dearborn, Michigan, where approximately 95% of my high school and middle school classmates were Arabs, I was used to talking openly about issues that impacted my people.

They asked me what I thought about something recently in the news that made Palestinians look like barbarians and my honest 19-year-old self replied, "Well, the media does not always portray the situation accurately." At the time, I thought, duh, everyone knows that. Everyone I grew up around knew that. Their eyes narrowed and they focused intently on my face, and the husband asked, "What do you mean, *exactly?*" I nonchalantly blurted, "Well, because the media is controlled by Zionists." Their eyebrows instantly flew up and I suddenly realized that I had said something wrong. They looked at each other knowingly and I instantly wished that I had said that I was Turkish or something less controversial. Moments later, I sat them and we exchanged quick fake smiles before I told them to enjoy their meals.

I spent the rest of the night quietly seating customers, flashing innocent smiles and avoiding conversations with nosey tourists. I guessed that they must be Jewish and supporters of Zionism—so maybe what I said hit a nerve?

The next day, I came in to work early to answer phones and clean menus. I strolled in to the sunny foyer and sat at a table near the bar. My manager walked in while I was wiping down the leather-bound wine menus. He was a big man—wide, about 100 pounds overweight and about 6 feet 5 inches—so it was easy for him to look intimidating. He knew this, so he tried to smile as much as possible to prevent fear and intimidation. As he came down the spiral staircase, he was not smiling. He moved purposefully towards me with a scowl plastered across his face. He sat down across from me and sternly asked me if there was anything I needed to tell him. I thought about all the free meals the cooks had given me for smiling sweetly at them or the toilet paper I had stolen last week and with my best innocent face replied, "Nope." Maybe I hadn't been smiling at our rich, white clientele enough; it wouldn't be the first time that I would be accused of being too serious.

He paused for a minute, searched my face, and then told me that he had just gotten a call from customers that dined with us the night before. I confessed that I had had a conversation that got "weird" but that I didn't think it was a big deal. I let him know that they had steered the conversation in that direction and that I was just responding to their questions honestly.

He looked at me intently, his face turning red and asked, "What did you say that made them angry?"

"I think it was something I said about the media and Zionists," I replied.

He raised his eyebrows, skeptical. "What about 9-11?"

I looked at him, confused. He then explained to me that the couple had said that I had condoned the events of 9-11 and condoned terrorist attacks in general. They told him that I should be fired and reported for suspicion of terrorism.

I froze, both confused and angry. I managed to convince him that it was not true, and luckily, he believed me, or at least appeared to. Later that day, after getting over the shock, I thought about why the couple would have made something like that up. I wondered when my olive skin and the word "Palestinian" had become a liability. Should I have avoided honesty when they asked where I was from, or kept the conversation light and "American?" I wondered about the future, how would I be able to avoid incidents like this—who could I trust to be honest about who I was and who could I have real conversations with? I was able to keep my job, but I had lost something else that I was not able to identify until many years and similar incidents later.

For years, I avoided controversial topics about the Middle East and even sometimes avoided telling people where my family is from. My brother and many other young men from my community had been picked up and questioned by the FBI for no reason besides that they were young, Arab-American men. I heard people talk about Arabs and Muslims in hateful ways before they realized I was one of them. I found that by just saying "Palestinian" or "Arab" or "Muslim," I apparently invite a political debate in which my "un-American" views will be put on the stand. I eventually learned how to adjust. 9-11 and the attitudes that followed it knocked the identity out of me for a time. I told people that I was from Detroit and that was it. I would maybe tell people that I was Middle Eastern, but that I was born in America. As a graduate student, I researched this phenomenon and found that many other Arabs were doing the same thing. We were changing our speech to make others comfortable and avoid confrontation. My own mother, who was born in Jerusalem, admitted to avoiding saying that she was Palestinian and instead saying that she is Jordanian. She was afraid of getting fired or being engaged in a conversation that would not end well. Now that I am aware, I don't live with the same fear, but I am still cautious. I know now that my words, beliefs and identity can get me into trouble and freedom of speech is only free if you have the right skin tone, and mine just happens to be a few shades too dark.

Chris is originally from Hawaii and spent most of his youth on the beaches of Oahu. He received his academic education through the University of Hawaii and is a school counselor. Chris currently provides his service part time to the students of Mira Costa Community College and full time to the youth incarcerated in the San Diego Juvenile Court system.

Chris
Maili Beach Park

This piece is dedicated to the people of the Hawaiian Sovereign Nation. May the land prosper in righteousness and set you free.

I was born and raised in Waianae, Hawaii, a place considered by many to be the pit of Hawaii. One way in and one way out, both figuratively and literally. It's definitely not the place that shows up on the Travel Channel. Many locals who were born and raised on Oahu have never been to Waianae. How can that be when the island is only so big? Tourists from all over the world come to Hawaii to enjoy the beauty and culture. It's the same beauty and culture that is celebrated on the west side, only it's authentic and not a show. Close to 80% of the Native Hawaiian population, the Kanaka Maoli people, live on the West Side. So why is the west so isolated?

Maybe everyone is scared of the stories. The stories of drugs, homelessness, violence, and crazy people. I'm not crazy or violent. I've done drugs, but I did most of it with rich people outside of my community. Homeless? What do you expect when the land is taken away from the people? Where there are rich, there are poor. Many of the Kanaka Maolis refuse to conform to a system of oppression that I will address later in this piece. Former President Bill Clinton wrote a letter apologizing for the forced annexation and overthrow of the queen, yet the land still remains outside of Hawaiian hands.

I remember as a kid playing with my friends at Maili Beach in Waianae, Hawaii. We walked in between rows of tents flying the Hawaiian State flag upside down while the Hawaiian sovereignty flag flew high above.

The British red, white, and blue flag was upside down while the flag with stripes of red, yellow, and green with paddle and oars in the middle, the sovereignty flag, was flying high with pride. The sovereignty flag is the symbol of the Kanaka Maoli, the true indigenous Hawaiians. I didn't understand it as a kid; all I knew was that they were poor and struggling, but proud. The friends I played with were always talking about who was more Hawaiian. We were as scrappy as can be—born fighters. We used to fight each other on the beach until only one stood tall with pride, king of Maili Beach. In the end, we helped each other up and we always had each other's back. We were family and that's what family does.

One hot Hawaiian morning, people ran down the street yelling, "They getting arrested, everybody getting taken away!" I didn't know what was going on, but being the nosey kolohe kid that I was, I jumped on my bike and peddled as fast as I could. When I arrived, Honolulu Police Department, HPD, had two buses parked by the beach. They were escorting all the moms, dads, aunties, and uncles who lived in tents on the beach, onto the bus. Child Protective Services, CPS, were taking my friends away. Babies cried loudly as they were held and taken by these strangers. There were groups of people from the community on the side-lines that were yelling, "Keep Hawaiian land in Hawaiian hands." "You have no right to take them, you crooks!" I remember noticing that some of the HPD officers and CPS workers were crying tears of shame as they took people away, while others smirked as if they were better than us. On the other side was a group of people chanting, "Ua mau ke ea o ka aina i ka pono. Ua mau ke ea o ka aina i ka pono. Ua mau ke ea o ka aina i ka pono." I didn't know the people, but what they said meant that the life of the land is perpetuated in righteousness. In other words, that all locals know the truth of who the rightful owners are, and that it is embedded in the Hawaiian state crest.

Soon after the buses arrived, the tents, along with my friends and other Kanaka Maoli people had been swept away. On the news they said,

"Operation Maili Beach Clean Up" was a success. Clean up? What do they mean by clean up and how do you call removing the people from their land a success?

Many were taken to shelters, while those who opposed were taken to jail. Most of my friends were put in foster placements or group homes because their families were deemed "unfit" to care for them by the state. From what my uncle told me, this wasn't the first time HDP would "clean up" the beach, and it would not be the last.

Slowly but surely the tents returned and the sovereignty flags flew again. This time it was a little different, or maybe it was the same, but I was the one who had changed. I was ten years older and now selling crystal methamphetamine, known on the islands as ice or batu. I was a teenager who thought he knew it all. I no longer went to Maili Beach Park to play, but instead, I went to Maili Beach Park to sell ice. The same beach park where my friends and I grew up playing. We sold to anyone and everyone. People from other communities with nice cars would often drive up, looking for ice. I used to get excited when girls from other communities drove up. Unfortunately, they weren't the only ones. We had friends drive up, aunties and uncles drive up; some even walked over from the tents. We were small time, just trying to be cool and make some money. It felt good to have money and all the attention that came with it.

Over the next six years, as I got hooked, ice destroyed me just like it destroyed my community. Like I said, we were just small time; there were bigger players involved. The family structure that was so strong and ingrained in the culture began to fall apart. Moms, dads, and several people my age were hooked. Ice brought violence to the community when dealers began to fight over territory. People that were hooked started to rob and steal to get the money necessary to get that high. The adults who used neglected their kids and exposed them to things that no kid should ever see. The ice epidemic in Hawaii was real and it hit the community of Waianae the hardest.

After going in and out of the system and everything that comes with that lifestyle, I made up my mind that I was done. I was sick and tired of the life I was living. I needed to go to college, at least that's what I remember my teacher saying back in high school. So, I went to LCC, Leeward Community College, aka Last Chance College, aka Losers Choice College. Whatever. It was college.

As a new college student, with a high school diploma that was not earned, and old habits and demons I was fighting, my pride restricted me from asking for help. I had a probation officer on my ass, a mind full of insecurities, no clue how to be a good student, a newborn baby, bills to pay and two jobs that I hated. I took eight years to get through community college, but I did it. I finished Leeward Community College and was off to the University of Hawaii. It's the university that has the saying "Ua mau ke ea o ka aina i ka pono" embedded on its school crest.

One of the first classes I took was Hawaiian Studies taught by Professor Kumu Kaeo. "I'm from Waianae," I thought, "this is going to be an easy class." The first day of class I learned that Kumu Kaeo was also from Waianae, so I knew for sure this class was going to be a breeze. I was dead wrong. Kumu Kaeo challenged and pushed me every day in ways that I had never experienced. With fists balled up and holding back the tears of frustration, I was ready to quit on several occasions, but I had come too far. The final exam wasn't a multiple-choice test; it was a presentation on a topic of your choice. For me, the topic was chosen and assigned by Kumu Kaeo. She handed me a video and a phone number. She said to watch the video and call the number. I went to my friend's house and watched the video. It was a video on Bumpy Kanahele and Haunani-Kay Trask. In 1994 Bumpy rallied 300 Kanaka Maolis and took over Makapuu Beach. They camped out and forced a negotiation. He negotiated with the state of Hawaii and settled peacefully for 45 acres of Hawaiian land on a 55-year lease for $3,000 a year. Years later, Bumpy was arrested on the land for interfering with a federal investigation. Three months

into his sentence the governor gave him a pardon. Bumpy is a legend in
Hawaii and gave people hope for a better Hawaii. Haunani Kay-Task is a
scholarly academic type, originally from California. She is a professor at
the University of Hawaii in the Hawaiian Studies department. Haunani
has led several protests against the military and tourism in Hawaii. Her
belief is that the U.S. is the enemy. She appears on the news regularly and
is considered an extremist by many. So here I was, thinking about a local
activist hero and a radical activist professor.

My mind was now spinning full of guilt and shame for the ice I had
sold, the houses I had broken into, for contributing to the problems of
my community and not being part of the solution. I now had to call the
number. I hoped it wasn't Bumpy or Haunani because I couldn't handle
that. It turned out to be someone from OHA, the Office of Hawaiian
Affairs. I was off the hook.

I met up with the guy from the Office of Hawaiian Affairs at Zippy's,
a local restaurant. He was a short Japanese guy and he spoke about the
need for compliance to meet state and federal laws, but at the same time
working with the community to build these efforts collaboratively. It was
extremely complicated as he talked about the law and legislation. The
more he talked, the more I got confused. When I asked questions, he
threw them back at me. It was as if he was looking to me for a solution.
The deeper I got into it, the more I couldn't figure out the right answer,
but at the same time I learned the politics of the situation from the OHA
point of view.

I presented the information and topic I was assigned—Hawaiian
sovereignty. It went well and I ended up getting a "B" in the class. She
just wouldn't give me that "A." At the end of class, Kumu announced
that she was holding a paina, a party, at her house for all of us. I scraped
some money together, bought some huli huli chicken, and went over to
her house. When I arrived, everybody was drinking, eating, singing, and
having a good time. I found Kumu and a quiet corner to talk. She said, "I

was hard on you because you are from Waianae. I could have given you a topic like hula or surfing, but I chose to give you Hawaiian sovereignty because you are part of the community." She stood less than five feet tall, with bloodshot eyes, and long wavy hair down to her knees.

Kumu, a professor at the University of Hawaii, represents our native land, Waianae, to the fullest. I never expected a teacher to have that kind of impact on me. Because of her, I get it. I went on to earn my master's degree in counseling psychology with an emphasis in school counseling. I returned to Maili Beach Park not as a clueless kid playing and fighting. Not as a senseless teen selling, using, and committing crimes. I returned as a community member who appreciates, values, and embraces the people of the land.

—*Ua mau ke ea o ka aina i ka pono.*—

Photo: Sarah Loud

Tatiana García was born and raised in the San Diego community of Logan Heights, where she learned the struggles her family and community face. She graduated from San Diego State University with her bachelor's in social work in May 2016. Tatiana has experience working with inner-city youth, unaccompanied child migrants, and organizing youth in Costa Rica. She plans to dedicate her life to empowering communities, especially youth, to organize and work to change their circumstances.

Tatiana García
Dear Daddy

I would like to dedicate this piece to all fathers and daughters, so we can be united.

We grow up as innocent little girls, in a world where boys are valued more than girls. Boys make their own standards, while girls have standards created for them. A boy wants to be lazy; well, that's how boys are. A girl wants to be lazy; she's not fit for a man. A boy is bossy; he's a leader. A girl is bossy; she's a bitch. A boy sleeps around; he has to satisfy his needs, but the girl that sleeps with him is now unclean. These are only a few double standards.

In all matters, boys are valued more by you, Dad. Sons are treated differently than daughters. Brothers are ultimately superior to sisters. Brothers make mistakes, and are forgiven. Sisters make one mistake, and the world has almost ended.

This letter is written to you, Dad, because I want you to hear my pain. I'm trying to tell you that I'm hurt, but you're too offended by my defensive stance. I threaten your position as a "man."

Look, I know you hate when I say this, and if I want to piss you off, I know that this is how to do it: "Dad, you treat my brother better." You and I both know it's true. Everyone sees it except you.

My brothers had your respect from the beginning. I've had to be relentless in my fight for mine. My brother has grown to be a good man, but he's had your help along the way. Two felonies and two misdemeanors down, and you were always there to bail him out. I've done four years at a university with a scholarship to help me out, and a loan worth less than his bail, which you paid, yet my student debt I must pay for myself. Daddy, you and I both know that our relationship has been a struggle. I hate recounting these moments. They reopen scabs and remind me of what was—but these scabs need disinfecting.

I can't pinpoint exactly where we went wrong, when we went from best friends to barely getting along. I didn't address the issue because I had yet to find my voice. I swept it under the rug with not much choice. A child forgives and just hopes for a better day, until that child grows up to learn what's what. I became an adult, and the dust under the rug began to show.

But let's take a moment to reflect; let's go back and see how things changed. It was when I was in elementary school. You had your bursts of drunkenness and you took your anger out on me. I remember the moments clearly. How can I forget the day you told me that you never wanted to see me. I remember mi abuelita and abuelito trying to calm you down while I lay in their bed crying, as I heard you deny me.

I was hoping you would change your mind, but you didn't. So I would live with my mother, and you'd never see me again, if what you said was true. At this time, I was only seven. I didn't understand why you wanted to get rid of me; all I wanted was to live with Daddy and watch the leprechaun movies Mommy told me not to watch because they gave me bad dreams. I would have done anything to feel you hug me.

But now it all makes sense, because when I was seven, my mom officially dissolved your marriage. You lost your wife, and when you looked into my eyes, I was a constant reminder.

Soon, I was in middle school. I was young and didn't know how to interpret your back and forth. You spent a lot of time in the garage, thinking, with a smoke in one hand and a drink in the other. "Dad, what are you doing? Dad, what are you thinking?" I never got an answer. "Go inside," is what you always told me. Until the day you had me sit on your lap. "What's wrong?" you asked me. "I don't want to lose you like we lost abuelito," I confessed. You tried to reassure me, "You won't. Abuelito was worse than me." Although the doubt in your voice was hard to mask, you knew it was enough to silence me, temporarily.

For years, Fridays were our father/daughter days. Ultra Star Cinema was our spot. An order of nachos, a garlic parmesan pretzel, and a large soda is what we got. We'd watch *Saw* every time a new one came out, or any funny movie with Will Farrell; *Anchor Man* and *Talladega Nights* were your favorites. But those times are long gone.

Your focus was on my brother, who moved out and got in trouble. He got arrested for the first time and got his girlfriend pregnant around the same time. You didn't get mad. What could you say? You had had him at the same age. Not too long after, he dropped out of high school. His ten years playing football ended in a second.

Before you knew it, I was in high school and I was dating the pastor's kid. I grew up with him and you knew the pastor well. I was at church three times a week and curfew was at 11. I grew up a bit, but I was still Daddy's girl. I was good and I still answered to you. And I would have done anything to get to spend time with you.

We always made plans a week in advance and I would call you the day before to make sure. But maybe that was my flaw; I tried to claim my time with you and to guarantee you would show up. But I guess that only got my hopes up. The day would come and I'd be anxiously waiting for you. I'd call you and you'd say, "I'll be right there. I'm on my way." I'd wait.… And an hour later, you were still not there. I'd call again; you'd say, "I'm coming right now." Red flag.

But despite everything, I still believed what you said. "Right now" never came, and I would call again. This time your phone just rang. "You have reached the voicemail of.…" I'd hang up and try again. Sometimes you answered with a slur, "I'm coming. I'm coming." But most of the time your voicemail listened better than you. The bar required your attention more than I did. And people wonder why I don't trust the word of a man. Grandma would always tell me, "No sé por qué siempre le crees. Ya sabes que no va venir." I don't know why you always believe him. You already know he's not coming. "No sé por qué lo esperas. Ya lo conoces." I don't know why you wait for him. You already know him. And she was right. You didn't come. You didn't call back, and I did know you, but I always had faith that one day I would say: I underestimated you.

Night would fall and I would stop calling you and go to bed. Eventually, you'd get home and kiss me on the forehead. Daddy, every time, I stayed up out of fear that you wouldn't make it home. The moment you walked through my bedroom door, I pretended to be asleep. I didn't want to face you because I was too hurt and didn't want you to see the tears running down my face. Once you kissed me and said, "I love you, honey," I was at peace. I couldn't be mad at you for standing me up because I was so relieved that you got home safely. In the end, your safety mattered more to me than my own hurt feelings.

A child always forgives and hopes for a better day; that's why I'd try again the next day. I always thought that tomorrow would be a clean slate, even though you never said sorry. Maybe it's because you knew that I had already forgiven you.

Then the time came for me to go to college. My freedom was your end. I moved out at 18 and never looked back. I think you realized that you couldn't cage a bird once it found freedom. Once a bird learns to use its wings, it depends on its own ability to fly and to survive. I shocked you and took you by storm. Your baby wasn't a little girl anymore. My wings weren't taking me back home anymore. I stopped waiting. I stopped calling. But I never stopped hoping. You thought I gave up on you, but all I did was stop you from opening more wounds.

Your daughter did as she pleased and didn't ask for permission. Curfew was no longer 11, and this disturbed your sleep. I know, because now you were calling me. Now it was my voicemail that listened to your angry plea.

My independence scared you because you knew that your daughter wouldn't be in bed waiting for you to kiss her forehead. You started to miss these things, and it started to make you question your purpose.

But unlike me, you didn't stay quiet. You would argue, cuss, and insult, because now, little birdie had found her voice. You threatened me with the things you still controlled, or thought would control me—my phone, my car, and my physical wellbeing. But nothing broke me. Not even when you told me that I'd never be enough. Not even when you threatened to hit me. What surprised you was my response: "I'll be the first to call the cops on your ass if you ever lay your hands on me." You said, "Oh, it's like that?" "Yeah," I said, "it's like that." You never laid your hands on me growing up, and I wasn't gonna let you start as an adult.

No matter what threat, I didn't break. I didn't argue, I simply demanded respect. I didn't *need* my daddy anymore. I *wanted* my father, but I wasn't going to be threatened or be disrespected, and I sure as hell wasn't going to sacrifice my self-worth.

We've come a long way since then. I know you remember the movies because you still bring them up to this day. You say, "I might just go to the movies alone," in hopes that I'll say, "I'm on my way."

For three years, I have lived on my own, and you were never invited into my home, but today, my door is open. I love you Daddy, but I just want you to understand me, love me for my individuality, and be happy that I'm stronger than you thought I'd be. Be proud of me, Daddy. I'm getting a degree for you, my mom, and my family. Now let's go watch a movie on Friday night.

Kristie Harris has lived on both the East and West Coasts but finds San Diego to be "home." She has primarily worked in public education. Kristie is currently finishing her bachelor's degree in organizational leadership through Southern New Hampshire University online. She enjoys spending time with her family and close friends and is passionate about the future of society's youth.

Kristie Harris
My Devil

This piece is dedicated to my family for being strong enough to fight off their devils and remain on the path to success.

That night their yelling and fighting began as it always did. The verbal abuse was loud enough to hear all the way down the hall and up the stairs to the bedroom I shared with my older sister, Trinity. I couldn't really pinpoint the happenings below us but I knew (as usual) it wasn't good. After a lot of banging, crying and violent movement my mom yelled, "Girls hurry! Come get in the car!" My sister and I looked at each other lying in our shared bed. I could see the fear in her eyes and she saw the same in mine. My sister, my second mom, as I've grown to call her, reassured me we'd be okay as we hopped out of bed in our nightgowns and ran down the stairs and out the front door.

The next thing I knew, I was in the car with my oldest sister, Michelle, who is blind, Trinity, my middle sister, my mom and myself, the baby of the family.

My mom drove in a state of panic, makeup-stained tears streaming down her face while she calmly told us everything was fine and not to worry. As we pulled up to her best friend Barbara's house to seek refuge from the violence and fear-stricken night, a figure suddenly appeared looming in the night sky in front of the car. It was a tall, dark man, with a long black cloak. His entire body was engulfed in a luminous red glow; it was my dad, and he was the devil. Mom stopped short of saying, "Shit, he's here!" as she quickly threw the car in reverse and tore down the street to the next house. He appeared again and again and again.

We made it to our final destination, a small, light-green house with four wooden steps that led to a small porch. This time, the devil was nowhere in sight when we arrived. We jumped out of the car, my mom in front leading Michelle, Trinity next, then myself. With my mom at the door and my sisters on the stairs, and me ready to put my foot on the first step, I looked to the right and there he was, my dad, the devil, quickly floating toward us, toward me! Terrified, but trying to hasten my step, I reached step two, step three; everyone else had made it into the house, but I was one step and a small porch away from safety. As I glanced over at him looming in the air next to me, my foot landed on the fourth step and the step broke. My foot got caught amid the cracked, splintered wood and I was within his grasp; the devil caught me.

Then, I woke up.

See, I had this recurring nightmare for years, about three to be specific. To the outside world, on any given day, our family was happy, but by night our home was filled with terror.

Over the next few years, the nightmares continued, as did the abuse. I trusted my mom, and I knew she was just defending herself and protecting us from the evil, not provoking fights or egging anything on. I knew her as my protector, as our protector, and I knew him for the mean, scary beast he was. I can still feel the lump in my throat that would form when he was around. It was a lump composed of fear; and in hindsight, it was probably made of anger and lack of understanding. He, in fact, was my biggest fear, my recurring nightmare, and he remained so for those few years.

Fast forward to the summer of 1989. My mom, my sisters and I were settling into our new town 3,000 miles away from "home" or hell, as I like to call it. We had run away from the devil a few months earlier and were starting over. It seemed like my nightmares had left me both in real life and in my dreams at some point after our departure.

As I hit dating age, being somewhat of a feminine tomboy, I tended to befriend the fellas easily. I landed my high school sweetheart, and he was white. Eventually, I met the father of my children, also white. I basically opted out of dating blacks. At the risk of sounding prejudiced, throughout my years growing up I had plenty of black friends, black male interests and so on, but I never let the men in. I suppose somewhere in my psyche, these men were all my dad, the devil. Admittedly, I believed for years that their kindness was only surface deep. As a young adult, I faced questions like, "Why don't you date your own race?" and my simple reply was, "It's just not my preference."

At about the age of 29 I met a man that really opened my eyes. During a conversation about racism, which I firmly THOUGHT I stood against, he asked a pointed question. "How can you stand so firmly against prejudices but you won't even give a single black man a chance? You are prejudiced." Ouch, I thought, that one hurt. Then the question, "Why don't you date black men, really?" I confessed that the man who should've been my savior, my example of a man, my protector, my hero was instead my devil, and I wasn't going to let that happen again. I remember he laughed at me and said I couldn't judge an entire race of men based on my father's flaws. He was only one man.

The conversation opened my eyes: maybe I was ready to seek a deeper understanding of myself and what I stood for; or maybe, he just used the right words to get through my thick skin. Either way, the conversation shamed me and made me question how I could advocate for equality and try to reason with people about their prejudices when I was still holding onto my own devil.

I did start expanding my dating options, and the first black man I really dated ended up just like my dad. As I left that short-lived relationship, I had feelings of animosity and was extremely angry and upset with his actions and with myself.

That's when the light bulb turned on. Hell, I've met the same devil before, the same man who regularly mistreated women, and he surely wasn't black. In fact, I'd met varying pieces of him numerous times, not all in one person perhaps, but none of them were black, not one.

I changed my single story of a black man and began working on myself. So here I sit, next to my favorite man who resembles none of my devils or demons, and he's black.

Photo: Sarah Loud

Aaron Harvey is dedicated to organizing in Southeast San Diego against the criminalization of the black community that is accomplished through gang documentation, gang injunctions, and gang conspiracy laws. Harvey's own documentation (as a gang member) and prosecution by San Diego's district attorney, Bonny Dumanis, inspired his activism.

In the summer of 2014, Harvey, along with dozens of other black men from his community, was charged with an untested law. Penal Code 182.5, what some are now calling the Lynch Code, is a gang conspiracy law passed by voters through a ballot initiative in 2000. The penal code says, in essence, that any documented gang member can be held responsible for any crime the gang commits, even if that individual had no knowledge of that crime.

It was a 7-month legal battle to get Harvey and his co-defendants released from jail. Once the charges were dropped, Harvey dedicated himself to the fight against the criminalization of his African American culture and to advocate for change in the fundamentally racist criminal "justice" system.

Now, a full-time student at San Diego City College, Harvey also works with Pillars of the Community in Southeast San Diego, to organize the formerly incarcerated against unjust laws and systems.

Aaron Harvey
The Other Side

To Dwayne and Kelly Harvey, for their love birthed a movement,
#SD33.

"Mom, do I have to go?"

"Yes boy, now shut up and go put on your shoes."

"I hate going down there," I mumble under my breath as I walk away pouting. That's Kelly, my mom, and it's day four of my uncle's trial. The charge: murder of a police officer. His name is Kyle, and he's my mother's younger and only brother. The drive down to the courthouse seemed to take forever and waiting in line to enter felt like an eternity. I hated everything about that place—the smell, the people, and the uncomfortable squeaky chairs. Nine in the morning until four in the afternoon, every day, with only an hour break. Hot Cheetos and Frito's Cheese Dip for lunch was the only highlight of the day. I just didn't understand why I had to go. Why couldn't I stay with Grammy? At least I'd be able to play outside or go swimming in the pool, even watch some TV.

As we took our seats in the courtroom, I heard him walk in before I could see him. The sound of chains clinking together reminded me of the killer zombies in the movies, creeping around the corner. He scuffled along because his ankles were chained, and his hands and arms were close to his body because his hands were chained too. The all-blue, too-small, faded jumpsuit reminded me of the one Houdini, the neighborhood house painter, would wear. I bet my life Uncle Kyle wished he could disappear like the famous Houdini right now. With his head hanging low in shame, and his skin pale from lack of sunlight, he'd sit down so the deputy could un-cuff one hand to re-cuff it to the chair. Each day, he would look up and his eyes would sweep across the courtroom, like a frightened child lost in the park, frantically searching for his parents. We would make eye contact, and he would smile with a grin so big you could see all his teeth, especially the front gold tooth with the "K" in the middle. He'd raise his hand in an "L" shape to me, and I'd mimic the letter with my small hand. I didn't know why, but that's how he'd greet me every day. I just thought that's what you did when you said hello. But I soon found out.

SMACK! The sound made by my mother's hand connecting to the back of my head.

"You want to be in here like your uncle? I bet not see you do that again." If looks could kill, my uncle would be dead from the scowl on her face. He'd laugh, and so would I. That turned into our little ritual every morning.

"All rise!" the deputy would say before the judge walked in, and for the next six hours I would be forced to listen to statements made by the district attorney, police officers and detectives about how much of a monster my uncle was: how he and his childhood friends sold drugs, killed people who didn't pay, and were now on trial for the murder of a police officer. All of that never made any sense to me because the uncle I knew wasn't a monster at all. What kind of monster would always give you money when you asked for it, let you play with the switches in his Cadillac and buy you clothes and toys? It just didn't make any sense to me. It enraged me that they would say these things. I'd try my hardest to fall asleep or ignore this continuous assault on my uncle's humanity, but it would pierce my ears like the slap my mother had delivered a few hours before.

Four o'clock couldn't come fast enough, but the day wasn't over just yet. Now we'd go visit him. I hated this part even more.

"We just saw him," I mumbled, but there was no use in complaining because I knew it would fall on deaf ears. The reception area of the county jail smelled like death to me; everything was dirty and old. The deputies searched my mom but never me before we walked to the odd phone booths—a thick glass window separated us from him and the telephone was on the hook. The cold metal benches were so uncomfortable to sit on. My uncle was always there before us, waiting, looking anxious and tired, and I grabbed the phone first.

"What's up, Lil G," he said.

"What's up, Big G," I replied. Our normal greetings were followed by the same questions every time.

"How's my nephew today?"

"Fine."

"You hear that bullshit they were saying about me today?"

"Yes."

"Do you believe it?"

"No."

"Okay, good. Now if you need some money to buy something, tell Ted to give it to you." Ted was my uncle's close friend who would give me anything I asked for while my uncle was away.

"Anyone picking on you out there?"

"No."

"What do you do if they are?"

That was my cue to put the phone down and start swinging as fast as I could. He would laugh so hard. My mother wasn't too pleased with that. She'd grab the phone and yell at him.

"Do you want him in here with you? That's not funny. Now say goodbye to your uncle so we can talk."

"Bye, Big G."

"Alright, little homey."

"Hey, what's wrong with your eye?" I noticed a scar on his face that I hadn't seen earlier at court that day.

"Playing basketball and this fool elbowed me." I could see on his face that he was lying, but I left it alone and handed my mother the phone.

"How they treating you in here?" I have never forgotten the look of pain and fear on her face.

Fast forward.

"Ay, CO, am I getting a visit today?"

"No."

"Ay, CO, can I make a phone call? I have court tomorrow and I want to remind my people to be there."

"Not my problem."

"Ay, CO, did I get mail today?"

"Yes."

He is so happy, for that letter reminds him that he is not totally disconnected from the outside world. He's facing fifty-six years to life in prison, on top of the fights and riots he has to deal with in jail, and he's thinking about letters, visits, and phone calls? I guess the biggest fear of being in jail is being forgotten about. He lies back on the cold, hard bunk and mentally rehashes the conversation with his attorney earlier that day.

"Life in prison! How the hell can I get life in prison and I ain't even did *shit!*"

His attorney's response was, "Look man, either sign for ten years or walk in that court room tomorrow and take your chances."

Scared as all hell, he decides to roll the dice and take his chances. Just before he passes out, his last thoughts are to hope his family comes to court.

CLACK! CLACK! The sound he wakes up to every morning is the sound of his cell door popping open, reminding him it's four a.m. and another day in court. Thirty bodies wait in a tank to be chained and bused to the courthouse. Usually nobody talks, but everybody tries to stay awake. Nobody sleeps in the tanks 'cause that's how you get jumped on or even worse, stabbed. Race riots are always popping off.

"What's up, fool? You on that murder case?"

"Yeh, why?"

The brother says nothing, hands him a piece of paper and walks away. Just then the guards walk in yelling.

"Everyone up against the wall, the bus is here." With no time to read the note, he throws it in his mouth before the guard walks by. Chained at the hands and feet he thinks, How the hell am I going to keep this thing from getting wet? The bus ride sucks; he's chained two by two and the A/C is on high, but he's happy to just see the outside. The county jail is underground so you never get to see the sun.

Once they are off the bus, unchained, and in the next holding tank, he hopes this note isn't too wet to read. He opens it and reads:

"WATCH THE WOODS ON THE WAY BACK!"

He thinks to himself, what the fuck does that mean? Could the whites be plotting to start a race riot in the tank on the way back? Not only is he fighting for his freedom in court, but now he has to fight for his life in just a few hours? The guard chains him yet again for court.

He scuffles into the courtroom, head hanging down low, trying not to take big steps because of the ankle chains. He hopes his family comes; this could be the last time he ever gets to see them. After searching frantically, he spots them and the sight of the familiar faces brings a huge smile to his face. It's next to impossible to concentrate on the testimonies when you're more worried about the knives waiting on you in the next tank.

The walk from the courtroom to the tank feels more like the Green Mile, kill or be killed; it's you or me. In a cage like an animal, better start acting like one. His head fills with the pump-up thoughts to prepare for the unknown waiting ahead. His heart beats fast, his palms sweat, his throat is dry. His last thoughts are: please God I don't want to die.

CLACK! CLACK! The holding tank door slides open and timidly he walks in. BANG! The door slams behind him and it's eerily silent. The blacks are up against one wall and whites on the other. Instantly both sides rush towards each other like a scene from an old civil war movie. Black and white bodies collide, punching, grabbing, kicking, and then...it stops, no guards no nothing, it just stops. What seemed like twenty seconds really lasted five minutes. He guesses they all just got tired. They check each other for wounds even though the adrenaline is still running high.

"Damn man, he got you good. Your eye is swelling up already," one of the blacks said, laughing.

Shit, I think, what am I going to tell my family when they come visit me?

"Thank, God I'm alive," I mumble as they're all being bused back to the jails.

"You have a visit!" the deputy yells. Excited, I jump up and head down the hall to the visiting rooms. I hope my eye isn't too noticeable as I wait anxiously on the other side of the glass and pick up the phone.

"Aaron what happened to your eye? It wasn't like that earlier at court." Kelly says.

Without even thinking, I say, "Playing basketball, and some fool elbowed me." Immediately the look on my mother's face seemed so familiar to me, the look of fear and terror. The look I was never able to forget.

The sound of chains clinking together will always depress my spirit and fill me with great horror. I often find myself in tears at the sound and sight of my fellow man confined in them. To that sight and sound I trace back to my first conception of the dehumanizing effects of modern day slavery. I can never rid myself of that look of terror on my mother's face seeing my uncle and then me in this state. The nightmares still haunt me and deepen my hatred of this heinous system, but strengthen my sympathies for the mothers with children in bondage.

Gabrielle Hines was born and raised in Southeast San Diego. Growing up, college was never an option she thought about. However, after converting to Islam she developed a love for knowledge and has recently graduated with her Bachelor of Arts in sociology.

Gabrielle Hines
Transitions

> *I dedicate this story to my cousin, Shay Anderson, and all others who have instilled in me a love for knowledge and have guided me through my college journey.*

I grew up with my two brothers, in a broken home, living mostly with my dad. The memories still knock at my door like an eviction notice. Being homeless has really shown me what the world looks like. The first time we got evicted, I remember feeling confused. Who were the marshals and how could they kick us out of our home? We ended up at St. Vincent de Paul, a shelter in downtown San Diego. Our first night there, we slept in an open space with other families. Before I went to sleep, I had all these thoughts. Why are we here? How come we are sleeping in a room full of strangers? What did it mean to be evicted? But when we went to breakfast the next morning, I remember looking at all the different food laid out and being happy. As our faces lit up, I told my brother that it looked like Hometown Buffet and that we could have all the milk we wanted. We spent a lot of our life living in cockroach- and rat-infested hotels. Drugs became the norm. No food became the norm. Yelling and cursing were routine. I don't have too many memories of my mom, even though I've tried many times over the years to conjure them up. Unfortunately, few exist because for most of our lives, she has been incarcerated or running the streets.

By the time I was 13, we were living in Southeast San Diego in the "brook," the home of the Piru Bloods. Everything was starting to go down the drain. My dad was on drugs. I failed most of my eighth grade classes and on top of that I felt like I could no longer be a child. I was forced to be an adult in order to take care of my brothers. Actually, for most of my life I've always felt that I had to be the adult even when my dad was not on drugs because he was never emotionally there. I know that my dad loved us but he didn't know how to show it, and when you're on drugs the only thing that you're thinking about is your next high. He spent a lot of time locked up in his room getting high with his friends and our relatives. Those relatives would sometimes give me money to buy food. I would take ten dollars and buy what I could. There were times when I didn't know what we were going to eat, so I asked relatives for money to buy food. My dad had too much pride to ask for help, and if he found out that I was asking or that relatives were giving me money he would yell and curse at me. Being the oldest in the house, I had to step up to the plate. When we didn't have money, I would do what I needed to do to make sure we survived. I would even hand-wash our clothes in the bathtub and hang dry them around the house when we didn't have money to wash our clothes in the coin machines.

Eventually I went to Illinois with the intention to visit my cousin Shay-Shay for the summer. When I first got to Illinois, I wanted to go back home. I missed my brothers, but somehow I decided to stay in Illinois. I knew what I would be going back to. My dad stayed locked in his room and didn't seem to care about how we were going to eat and whether we had clean clothes or not. I couldn't hold my brothers with my 13-year-old hands.

Staying with my cousin Shay-Shay has had a major impact on my life. Growing up I never experienced what a true family structure felt like until I went to Illinois. My cousin is someone who comes from where I come from and yet was able to change her reality after converting to Islam. I got to see her build a life with her husband. They worked together, raising their kids peacefully and that was something I admired because it was something I wasn't used to. I wanted that for myself. They were filled with so much light and love and I know that being Muslim was the cause of that change. Living with my cousin I got to witness the true essence of Islam through actions and character. I saw her teaching her children and emphasizing education and that sparked a desire in me to seek knowledge. We studied and read almost every night, which was new to me, and after I became Muslim, I was thirsty for knowledge.

I eventually came back home to San Diego to live. I remember running up the stairs that led to my dad's apartment. I was excited because I had not seen my brothers in almost two years. I walked in the door, and my cousin was sitting on the couch with his girlfriend. As I walked through the doorway, he said to me, "Ew! You're ugly. What did Shay-Shay do to you? You look like a fucking Somalian!" I was wearing hijab, a headscarf and symbol of Islam. During this time a lot of Somalis were moving into our neighborhood, so my cousin associated Islam and hijab with Somalis. They associated hijab and Islam as something foreign and, therefore, ugly. Their attitude left me sad and confused—how could they hate something that I loved so much?

My brothers were not home; they must have been outside playing. As I unpacked my stuff, I thought about all my family and friends that I wanted to see, but what would they think? What would they say? How would they react? Would they react like my cousin did? Would they think that I was trying to be something other than myself? Would they think that I've adopted another culture?

Growing up, I sometimes felt like an outsider. My mother is Filipino and my father is black. I remember being teased. I was called "gook" by family and friends. Although it may have been said jokingly, it always struck a chord with me. My ancestors came to this country as slaves (enslaved Africans) who were stripped of their names, identity, culture and religion, so sometimes we have the tendency to adopt or create another culture. You become like an orphaned child not knowing who you are or where you come from. The trauma of identity struggle is something that I've always known and there I was, 15 years old, rocking hijab and long skirts, something that is foreign to my family and friends. This was a painful time for me. My dad would throw my hijabs and books away. He strongly opposed my choice to become a Muslim. My dad was once a member of the Nation of Islam, but his first wife became a Sunni Muslim (like I am) and divorced him after he decided to stay with the Nation of Islam; so I was left assuming that this is why he disliked Islam. How could someone hate something that I had come to love so much? This is something that I continue to struggle with till this day.

Eventually, I ended up living with my older sister, and although I was still living in San Diego, I felt as if I was leaving my little brothers again who were still living with my dad. While living with my sister, I started reading and studying more and came to realize that many regions of Africa and the Philippines had a strong Muslim presence. This information was something real, something tangible that I could hold on to. I found a connection between Islam and my heritage and realized that I didn't have to give up my culture; in fact, I started embracing it. All of our lives as African Americans, we adopt other cultures or create cultures that we call our own, but Islam is something I could connect to Africa and the Philippines. I felt like now, as a Muslim, I had direction and a sense of peace and I wanted to share that peace with others, such as friends and family. I felt love and sincerity in Islam which was missing in my own family.

Growing up I didn't see myself having a future and never saw the hope for an education. How do you believe in things that you have never seen? But I went back to school with a different perspective, with a desire to learn about everything. Somehow I was lucky to come across some people who saw potential in me. They knew I didn't have any guidance, so they stepped up to be that support system that I didn't have. It was my 12th grade year; I was graduating soon and my counselor started trying to encourage me to go to college and although the idea was something appealing to me, I had never thought about it before, being that none of my family had ever gone to college. I didn't know where to begin, but my counselor and others encouraged me and made me believe that I could do it. I write this story reflecting on the things that gave me that spark to want to learn and the people who reminded me to believe. Islam served as a catalyst to help me better understand my family, gave me a sense of direction and emphasized the importance of education, and now it is 2016 and I will be the first in my family to graduate with my bachelor's degree one week from today.

Kevin Bryce Jones is a native of San Diego who was born and raised in a neighborhood commonly referred to as "the Coast." Throughout his 35 years on the planet (Southeast), he has overcome poverty, the gangsta life and incarceration. He is a full-time single dad and a student at San Diego City College. Kevin has been blessed with the will to succeed.

Kevin Jones
The Moment That Changed Me

I dedicate all of my success to the principles instilled in me by my mother, Geraldine Burgess-Jimenez. May she rest in peace.

The weekend arrived and I was excited. No, not because there was no school or the fact that I could sleep late, but because my family was planning on taking a trip to my grandparents' house. It was a two-hour drive, one that my mom had been planning to take for a while. Brawley, California was probably one of the smallest towns in Cali. You could walk from one side of town to the other within a couple of hours. The country atmosphere was always something that I admired: farm animals, friendly people, good fishing, and my grandparents, of course. For a 13-year-old boy with five siblings, raised by a single parent, life was crazy in the early '90s. San Diego was where I was born and raised. As beautiful as San Diego is, Southeast was the flip side of that beauty. Southeast San Diego was split into four sections—Eastside, North Eastside (East Dago), the South and the Westside. This is where most of the minorities were corralled to live—the slums, the inner city, the ghetto. It was home; it was all I knew: the poverty, the struggle, the violence and the police. I was not really sure why the police were in this community other than to harass and brutalize on a regular basis. While living in Dago, the opportunity to visit a different place was a break, so those little trips to Brawley were something I loved to do with my fam. I did not, however, realize that this particular trip would change my view of life.

My mother, my Aunt Teresa, my sister and two brothers and I left early Saturday morning. My oldest sister stayed in Dago, because she had her own place with two children of her own. My oldest brother William also stayed, because he was in the Job Corps and wanted to hang out with his friends for the weekend. So we loaded my mom's minivan, and we hit the road. As I think back about that ride, something seemed out of place, though I shrugged it off. Maybe it was a premonition.

We hit the highway. There was music, a fully stocked ice chest, and lots of conversation. It had been about two years since our last road trip and everyone was happy to go and see my grandparents in my mom's hometown. By the time we hit Alpine, I was out cold, sleeping. I didn't wake up until we were 20 miles away from Imperial County.

We finally pulled into Brawley 15 minutes later and all the kids, me included, jumped up and raced into the house to greet our grandparents. There were big hugs all around. My cousin who lived with my grandparents was at work and I could not wait to see him; I thought he was a cool dude. He worked at the corner store. Being my entitled self, I went into his room since he wasn't there yet, while everyone else was mingling. I played with his trains; I knew how he felt about his train collection, so I was careful. To my surprise, he crept up on me, slammed me down on the bed and licked my face. This was all in fun but his breath smelled like old hot dog water and I had been slimed. Wet Willie always greeted us like this, so I accepted the treatment as always.

The trip was off to a great start; we ate, laughed and caught up on missed times together.

My cousin took us fishing the next day. We all hung out with some neighbors trading stories and relaxing until we had to get back on the road that evening.

I enjoyed every minute of that trip and was somewhat mad we had to leave. We packed up and left at about three in the afternoon, reaching San Diego at about five o'clock, right before it got dark. My mom dropped off my two brothers and me at home, while my sister rode with her to take my Auntie Teresa home.

The house was quiet and seemed eerie for some reason. I guess it was the calm before the storm. We were home for 15 to 20 minutes before I heard my little bro yell, "Get the fuck off of me." I laughed because I thought my brothers were just wrestling around as we often did. I was all smiles until I heard an unfamiliar voice yell, "Get on the ground! Don't move!" My heart raced as I ran to see the commotion, but I was cut short by a man wearing a mask and wielding a machine gun, yelling at me to freeze and get on the ground. I was slammed to the ground by another man and put in cuffs, still not understanding why this was happening. I recognized these people though; they were the police, but why were they here?

For reasons I cannot explain, the whole street was blocked off, and there were helicopters in the sky. I was amazed but confused at what prompted them to enter our house like that.

When my mom and sister returned to the house, the police finally released us from their SWAT vehicle. My mom was pissed, looking at us like, What in the hell did y'all do? I had seen that look before and I was like, I didn't do nothin'. A detective took us inside the house to explain. He asked us if we knew William Tolliver. My mom replied, "Yes, he's my son." She said, "Please don't tell me something happened to my son." The detective replied that they arrested him and his friend Dennis on Saturday for robbery and murder.

My brother was alive and that was a relief. It was his first time in trouble, and I thought they would give him probation or a small amount of time, but I was in for a shock.

My brother had a big heart. He was intelligent. He did not gang bang, and he was not a drug dealer. My brother was just a 20-year-old trying to make it out of a society that most men of color don't. So no matter what anyone said, I knew he would receive justice.

Naïve to the judicial system and unaware of what was to come, I was hopeful for the best outcome. I was aware of the famous American phrase: an individual is innocent until proven guilty. Little did I know my brother was already guilty of being poor, black and guilty until proven innocent. Soon, this moment in my family's life would shape the way I lived my life. I could not believe my oldest brother had been involved in something like this. Despite the statistics, my brother was the opposite of what the world painted young black males to be. I mean, yes, he was black and poor and from a place overwhelmed by poverty and violence, but my brother was not a killer or a thief!

After William was arrested, my whole family went down to the county jail to see him. Instantly the water works began. My mother erupted like a tidal wave of tears, sobbing with a look of worry that sent chills down my spine. She seemed to have aged overnight. Something clicked and I knew my brother's problem was too big for any one person to shoulder, but I was taught to always keep the faith and that things would work out for the better.

I love my bro. I didn't like him at times (you know, sibling rivalry), but nothing out of the norm. I shared a room with him; he taught me how to ride skateboards; everyone liked him. So I prayed, my mom prayed, the church prayed, and our friends prayed. At that time, I still felt that he would receive a fair trial. My brother was strong but you could see the worry in his face.

We attended court date after court date after court date. Two years later my brother's trial started and was over in two weeks. From my perspective, it was all bad from the gate. In hindsight, the DA was the biggest asshole I'd ever seen. He made my brother out to be the devil himself, even though his crimee gave a statement that William was not the one who killed the cab dispatcher; in fact, he was not even in the building at the time and had no knowledge that the murder was taking place. He was just a driver on a breaking and entering. During the trial my brother's public defender, or as I now call him, his public pretender, did not say much. I swear, even the judge seemed to be sleeping at times.

Maybe he was just resting his eyes but I doubt it. The jury did not waste any time deliberating; they came back the next day with a verdict. They found my brother guilty on conspiracy to commit murder and robbery with great bodily harm.

My brother was sentenced to a life in prison.

My faith in the justice system was lost that day. My mom's heart was broken, my brothers and sisters were grief-stricken and my family seemed incomplete. The feelings among us were indescribable. My brother was not dead but he was lost forever, in a place where one becomes a number and living is an everyday struggle. Nothing would ever be the same again. We would not wake up to my brother on holidays; we could not celebrate any of his birthdays with him. The worst part of it all was that he would never be free. He would pay his debt to society with his last breath and the world would just keep turning. While the world keeps turning, my view of the justice system will always be jaded.

Christopher Kennison represents the communities in Southeast San Diego of Chollas View/Mt. Hope and of the South Bay, Imperial Beach. Formerly incarcerated, he is a family man who is now building a better future for his kids through his work for social justice and helping out the community in a positive way.

Christopher Kennison
Free Mind, Imprisoned Body

> *I dedicate this story to my son Christopher John Kennison II, and my other kids, Lawrence and Kylamae; my big brother, Wilfredo Wilbur Dayandante; my future wife, J'kyla Faulkner; and, last but not least, to my mom and sisters, Nilda and Natalie Meyer. Also, to all my homies going through the struggle and my friends who are in the grave.*

I remember laying on my rack and the deputy saying, "You're going to be on the Thursday bus to prison." All I could think of was the judge telling me, "The jury has found you guilty of robbery, conspiracy to commit a crime and assault. I hereby sentence you to two years." I looked at my public defender, better known as a public pretender, because they never actually help you out. As usual, he was just sitting there working on his next case instead of mine. I saw the expression of shock and fear on my friends' and family's faces. At that moment, I couldn't even look at them. I put my head down, embarrassed and ashamed of letting everyone down. The feeling of being an outsider and a loser multiplied by the emptiness and loneliness came over me. My public defender said, "Look at it this way. You were looking at nine and a half years; consider two as a blessing. Plus you're young; you could walk it off." I told him to get out of my face. I shouldn't be doing no time at all. My police description was a Hispanic male, five feet, two inches, and 180 pounds. I am not Hispanic, I'm over six feet tall, and the last time I was 180 pounds, I was probably in the fifth grade.

That night, I eventually drifted off to sleep and at three in the morning a deputy's voice sounded over the intercom, "Kennison, pack up, you're going early." While I was getting my waist and wrist chained up to two other people, an older guy I knew from always going to court together told me, "Don't waste your life coming back and forth to this place. Don't trip, youngster. You're one step closer to home and your journey is almost over." I told myself he was right. No more going to court and wondering when I would go home. Now I just had to get this time over with. Looking around before I got on the bus I saw the nervousness on a lot of young men's faces, but we were all trying to mask it with that I-don't-care attitude. The key is to never show feelings of being scared— keep your fear on the inside. I knew I'd be all right because I knew how to conduct myself. I learned all this in the county jail and growing up on the streets. "You don't steal from others. If you gamble or borrow something, pay your debts; keep it a hundred, stay true, don't be something you're not, and always remain humble."

A lot of people just went to sleep on that bus, but I was not planning to sleep at all. I never got used to being chained up and packed like cattle, like slaves from the 1800s. I shook my head and looked out the window. Out there I saw people driving by, going along with their everyday lives. One man was mad about the traffic he was sitting in. I envied him at that moment. I would have done anything to be that person who hates waking up at 4:30 to go to a job they hate. I remember thinking that this person didn't know how easily his freedom could be snatched from him. At this point, my freedom had been snatched from me, and I couldn't do anything about it. It was a bad dream come true.

I was nervous as we approached the prison but you wouldn't know it by looking at me. My heart was beating faster and faster by the minute. The air conditioning on the bus felt like it was set at damn near below zero, but when I saw the prison I began to sweat. As we got inside I saw a sea of electric fences topped with barbwire and even more barbwire between them. I didn't know what to feel at that moment. I was just numb. When we pulled up into the receiving and release center (R & R), the correction officers rushed out like a pack of wolves. One of them said, "I don't care where you're from, we're the biggest gang here. You see, there are no cameras here, so if you want to give us problems, we will take care of the situation."

They stripped and searched us one at a time. I could never get used to the dehumanizing experience of standing next to other men who were also completely stripped down. It reminded me of the images of naked black bodies of men, women and children being inspected before being sold on an auction block.

I sat in the holding tank from eight in the morning to six in the evening with about 30 other men. We were fed once during this whole time and everybody could hear my stomach growling. When six o'clock finally came, we got to walk outside to our housing unit. The sun was still up and the sky was blue with few clouds in sight. I soaked in the sun, thinking they can take away everything else but they can't take away the sun and the sky. After that moment of happiness a sudden rush of loneliness overwhelmed me. I knew my family and friends were hurting that I was gone and couldn't be there for them. I hoped they thought of me as much as I thought about them. The scariest feeling of being locked up is being forgotten about and not cared for by anybody.

Before I got to the dorm a CO came out and said, "Welcome to your new home. Don't give me no crap and I won't give you none. When you walk to your racks, if you don't have a mattress, go find one. If there aren't any, tough luck. Ask tomorrow's shift for a mattress because I can't do nothing for you."

When he said that, I made it my goal to go find one 'cause I wasn't planning on sleeping on metal, and I'd seen people go without a mattress for days. As I walked in the building there were about 200 people; 60 to 70 were black. I recognized anger and despair on everybody's faces. Mad at the fact we were stuck here until we paid our so-called "debt to society" and when released, we had to give another three years of parole.

Looking from left to right, I saw whites helping whites and Hispanics doing the same with their own people. With the African Americans, it was the total opposite. Everybody would ask you where you from before they asked your name. People wouldn't even help me carry my bags. They would say, "There go your homeys. They could help you out." I was disgusted because I was tired of how we treated each other. At some point we went from having togetherness and solidarity to dividing up, looking at one another as an enemy or threat.

Prison was racially divided. We even had to share a shower with people of our own race. However, the very next day we had a moment of solidarity; all of the prisoners refused to get off their racks to eat, to go to school and even work. It felt good to stand up for ourselves to protest the dehumanizing conditions. Next thing I knew, an army of COs came in and forced us to strip down and sit on the cold metal tables. The captain came in and said, "We run the show here," but in actuality, I was sure that the prisoners ran the prison and the guards just worked there. Ironically, after his speech he called all the shot callers (representatives) from the different races to resolve the problem. One reason that we were protesting was because we couldn't exercise. They didn't want anybody working out. They would cheat us out of our yard and keep us locked in the dorm. On top of all that, we were malnourished. The whole month and a half I was at reception I lost 28 pounds doing absolutely nothing. Not much changed after that, except that they gave us a little bit more yard to ease some of the tension.

The next day out for yard the alarm went off, and when that happens, it means to get down. I didn't want to lie in the dirt so I tried to run to the concrete but it was too late. I was the last one down. A CO named Baker came up to me and tried to take my ID. He rushed me like a hawk on its prey. "Hey, give me your ID, Fat Ass. You're one dumb bastard; we could've shot your ass, boy." He was an old white officer that everyone told me to avoid and when he called me "boy," it felt as if we were in the

South in the 1960s. In his eyes I saw a fire that could burn down a forest. It was the same fire reflected in the eyes of white lynch mobs across the South. I could've given him my ID and swallowed my pride, but instead I chose to stand up for myself.

I said, "Come on, Baker, there's no reason for you to talk to me like that; won't you come at me with some respect. I ain't no boy! I'm a grown man and them slavery days is over. Come correct and I'll give you my ID."

"You really a dumb bastard, boy. I'm not asking you for your ID, I'm demanding it. With that attitude you'll be back in prison. Just another dumbass."

At this point I was fuming on the inside, so I threw my ID on the ground and told him to pick it up if he wanted it. Next thing I knew I was slammed to the ground so fast and his backup appeared out of thin air. I now knew why they said they were the biggest gang. They escorted me to a cage that was smaller than a telephone booth. I felt like an exhibit at the circus or an animal at the zoo. I was stripped down and left in there until the evening. I now couldn't buy food and was forced to eat the un-nutritious, artificial meals prepared by the prison. It was a cold day but I wasn't going to let them break my mind or soul.

I continued to have similar altercations with the COs at Wasco. I was deemed a problem, and in their eyes I didn't have rights. They wanted to get rid of me as soon as possible. I was classified faster than anyone and got sent to the California Correction Center in Susanville, California. The day I left it was way before sunrise, but what I remember most was they had us wearing jumpsuits made out of paper. A paper shirt and paper boxers. The state was cheap as hell. It was raining so we had to walk in the rain before we got on the bus. You could only imagine what happened to our jumpsuits then. It took about seven hours to get to Susanville, but the crazy thing is this prison is right across the street from *another* prison. When I saw that, I realized that this state is designed for a certain demographic of people to be incarcerated. Why do people let stuff like this go on? Could it be because people just don't know?

After being in Susanville for a while I got a job and was working as an electrical engineer, but they had me in the boiler room most of the time. Being in the boiler room was hazardous to my health because I was breathing in fumes and chemicals. I got paid 13 cents an hour. If you refuse to go to work, you'll get more time added to your sentence. Forced prison labor is the definition of modern-day slavery.

I remember one day the guards were unlocking doors for yard. I had two months left until I could go home. I didn't want to go outside, but my homey came by and asked me to come. I had a feeling in my stomach something was going to happen; I just felt it in the air. After about ten minutes a riot popped off. All the Crips from Long Beach, Compton and Watts rushed the Sacramento Bloods. It happened in the blink of an eye. I was literally 20 yards away from them on the baseball bleachers, watching. I saw people getting stomped out and faces getting kicked. People took out prison knives ready to poke anybody. The alarm was going off. COs were shooting tear gas and mace, yelling, "Everybody down!" The guards from the watchtower took out their mini-14s, ready to start shooting, but by then everyone was down.

We were handcuffed and laid out on the yard for hours in the hot sun on that summer day. I could feel the ligaments and the muscles in my arm tightening and burning up. I yelled at a CO I recognized named Olah who was a vet, so this wasn't new to him. I was yelling, "You know this isn't right; there are people with medical conditions. Someone could die out here." He replied, "Shut up. I don't care. Keep talking and watch what's going to happen." I kept talking as I was escorted to the gym to be examined by the doctors. They escorted 400 people that day so you could imagine how long it took. We were lucky it all happened before the three o'clock shift change because otherwise we would have been handcuffed till the following day. Once I got my turn to be examined, I was happy. I figured I was going back to the dorm, but I was wrong.

While I was getting checked, CO Olah came by and said, "He has marks consistent of being involved. Take him to the hole."

I yelled, "You know these marks are from the handcuffs and me leaning my back on the fence!"

"I don't care. Take it up with committee, but in the meantime, you're going to administrative segregation." (This place was better known as the "hole.")

The hole is basically a prison in a prison. All I got was more time. That two months I had left turned into five months. During that time, I was in the hole for almost four and a half months. I thought that was long, but there were people who'd been in there for years. My life in the hole was the same thing every day—24 hours a day in my cell, come out to yard for three hours a week and three showers a week, but most of the time, we got two. I hated being dirty so I bird-bathed every day. My cell was so hot my body dripped with sweat. The air conditioner didn't work. It was so hot you could heat the lunchmeat on the walls. The only thing that kept me sane was books. I read any book I could get my hands on. From my cell, I would try to get a glimpse of what the COs were watching during the day and night. One day as my stomach was growling from being so hungry, I realized I was wrong. They *could* take away the sun and the sky. For me and thousands of others, all we were left with were four walls and a light that was on for 18 hours a day that replaced our sun. I had a flashback of what that man had told me:

"Don't waste your life coming back and forth to this place." It is a place of misery, hopelessness, anguish and anger. This isn't for me.

Juanita "Joanie" López was born and raised in the San Diego community of Barrio Logan. Currently she is a student at San Diego City College where she is graduating with her AA in English and Chicana/o Studies with a certificate in Creative Writing. At SDCC, she has served as president of MEChA, as a writer and editor for *El Coyote/Crossing Borders Online Newsletter*, and she is a member of Pillars of the Community Scholars Society. She also served as one of the first members of the Barrio Logan Community Planning Group. In addition, she has been published in several publications where she writes family and cultural narratives and showcases her community through photography.

Juanita "Joanie" López
The Lasting Memories of Us

I dedicate this story to my brothers and our dad who is watching over us.

I heard an unfamiliar knock on my door. "Ahí voy!" my mom yelled and of course I followed right behind her. "Ey Consuelo, está mi papá?" a tall young man in his early twenties asked. "Se está bañando," my mom replied. My mom had always been a respectful and respected woman, and this young man addressed her with respect. Confused by what I had heard, I looked up at my mom. My dad was the one showering not him, I thought. "Entra," my mom said to this stranger as he sat down in our small, dimmed living room, which was full of Santos and different Virgen Marías. My dad came out and that's when I saw them hugging one another. "Mira, este es tu hermano Carlos," my dad said. Not only did I feel tiny next to this giant but I felt shy, so I smiled and giggled. Coming out of the room, I saw my little brother's eyes widened in surprise, wondering who this young man was hugging *our* dad. It felt funny saying that I had an older brother, for all I've ever known was that I only had my little brother Abel who was three years younger than me, and he was my best friend.

Days went by when Carlos showed up again, but this time he wasn't alone. He came back with José. José was older than Carlos. He had more meat on his bones than Carlos, that's for sure. José was nice and looked a lot like our dad. I thought he was a jokester because he used his Chicano slang a lot and his "me entiendes Mendez" would make me laugh, unlike Carlos who wouldn't say much. This time, my brothers came asking our dad for money. I never knew how much they asked for, but one thing I do remember clearly is that the three of them sat on the couch. Carlos and José had their long arms around my dad's shoulder with their faces looking directly at the camera with a prideful look because they were taking a picture with Pops. Dad was still wearing his work clothes, but he looked happy as they all posed as the Polaroid camera flashed. Their visit was one of the last ones, for they moved to Oxnard, California because their mother wanted to live near her brothers. She was a woman I had never met but whose name I began hearing in my house.

It was the summer of 1995 when my mom took Abel and me to Memorial Park because the Boys and Girls Club used to give out free lunches during the summer. As I waited in line to get the usual, a corn dog with a carton of apple juice and a piece of fruit, my mom whispered to me, "Mira, ella es tu Hermana," pointing to this tall, young, thick woman whose light brown curly hair was covered in a hair net. "Hola Consuelo, hola m'ija, yo soy tu hermana Laura," she said as she added an extra carton of apple juice as if that was her way of letting me know I was special. Our relationship afterwards didn't really flourish. I don't have many memories of doing anything with Laura until the summer of 1999 when she asked our dad if Abel and I could spend a few weeks in Oxnard. Dad surprisingly agreed. She knew that our dad wasn't the type to take us out to the park or have any type of fun. So Laura surprised us when she told us she was going to take us to Disneyland. I was thrilled because for the first time we bonded as a family.

Back in our upstairs apartment on Valle Avenue, my mom and dad argued daily. My dad was always yelling at my mom, complaining how I didn't know how to cook or clean, always comparing me to Laura. Apparently, by the age of five she already knew how to do everything a woman was supposed to do, such as clean the kitchen, wash clothes, cook, but not me, I was too busy playing house with my brother and not worrying about anything else. My dad's philosophy was, "I'm going to discipline these kids, because if I don't, they're going to be hooked on drugs like these other motherfuckers, or get pregnant como esta." Esta was Laura who got pregnant by the age of 15. So while my dad was becoming a dad again with me, he was also becoming a grandpa for the first time. Oftentimes, my dad would leave the house for hours to spend time with his grandchildren, but he never took Abel and me with him. But it was during this time that I remember hearing the word "drugs" a lot. I knew that drugs were bad because of the red D.A.R.E ribbon I wore in my kindergarten class, but I didn't know what drugs looked like. What I also didn't know then was that my brothers were drug addicts and they asked my dad for money to supply their bad habits. My parents' arguments had roots—his prior marriage and family was one of the many reasons my brothers got lost in their own little world. They felt hurt, betrayed, and jealous of Dad's new life, his new kids—me.

A new chapter began when our phone started to ring numerous times a week. One time my mom asked me to answer and that's when I heard, "You have a collect call from Carlos; to accept charges, press one." I didn't know what that meant, but my mom pressed one and handed the phone to my dad. My brother was doing time in prison.

One morning, my mom woke us up and we all got ready. We drove for what seemed forever, and I just remember seeing flat and empty surroundings, then mountains ahead of the road. When we reached our destination, our identifications were checked, and the security officer searched us to see if we had anything in our pockets. We all sat in the waiting room as we waited to be called. My mom remained in this cold room, as my little brother, Abel, Dad, and I went inside. We entered a gray-looking room that had glass windows with black telephone receivers. I waited anxiously and soon saw Carlos enter from the other room. He walked toward us with his head held high and sat down to face us. He greeted us with a huge smile but his toughness diminished as tears rolled down his cheeks. Both Carlos and Dad reached for their phone to talk to each other, and although they were happy to see each other, I could tell that seeing his son behind those glass walls upset my dad. I sat there listening to my dad and watching Carlos's mouth move. I might've said a few words to him, but I don't recall what I might've said; perhaps he asked how I was doing in school.

On another occasion the same routine happened, but this time we sat outside. It was a sunny day, and we all sat down on a red bench. Carlos brought a food tray with him and handed me a peanut butter and jelly sandwich with an orange juice, while he drank a carton of milk. It had been a long time since we shared any bodily contact, but this time we were able to hug and kiss each other. What I remember most from the visit was the location because I never forgot where I ate my very first P&J sandwich—it was in Donovan State Prison.

Another year went by after that visit to Donovan. It was in 1997 when my brother Carlos was released from prison. I think it was Thanksgiving because my mom had cooked her very first turkey. It wasn't the typical American turkey with stuffing served with mashed potatoes. No, my mom made it enchilado with chile chipotle and all kinds of other chiles with herbs and spices accompanied by Mexican rice and beans. My brother Carlos came over to eat. He was staying at my uncle's house across the street because he wanted to stay with my cousin instead of us. He ate and complimented my mom on the delicious meal. That's when I noticed that for once my mom felt appreciated by her stepson. Carlos decided to stay a bit longer after dinner. He called me over to sit down with him on the couch. He said, "Ey, come here, m'ija; they're gonna show la película del *Titanic*." *Titanic* was the biggest movie in theaters during this time and the Discovery Channel had a documentary of the actual boat sinking. My brother wrapped his long, tattooed arm around me and I remember outlining his Aztec designs that consisted of pyramids, Spanish conquistadors, and Aztec women whose breasts were exposed to my innocent eyes. He noticed my admiration for his tattoos, so he explained to me that the pyramid represented the prison he was in, and the Spanish conquistadors were the ones he had to fight; as for the Aztec women, they were the women important in his life, and I wondered if he would ever include me on his inked body. But what I remember the most from that night was looking at him and smiling at the fact that I was interested in his black beanie that had a rubber band tied in the back; and for once it felt nice having an older brother who was sitting with me at home and sharing stories, even if they were prison stories.

In the fall of 1999 our dad, Abel and I suffered a car accident. In that accident I became paralyzed from the waist down, my brother suffered minor injuries, and our dad lost his life. I spent three months in the hospital recuperating but in those three months a lot of other stuff happened too. My dad was buried and I wasn't able to attend his burial because I was having surgery. I recall seeing my brothers at the hospital and asking how I was doing. Laura came to see me before heading back to Oxnard; she placed her hand over my forehead and told me how much she loved me, and she reassured me that everything was going to be okay. When I was released from the hospital, I was bound to a wheelchair, and my mom had become a single mother to a seven-year-old boy and a nine-year-old girl.

During these difficult times, I yearned for a father figure. I thought that my brothers were going to move to San Diego to be closer to us but that didn't happen. Instead, they got themselves in trouble with the law once again and back to prison they went. My brother Carlos wrote to me a day before my birthday. He sent me a birthday card, and I remember being so happy even though I could barely understand his horrible handwriting. Inside my card was another Polaroid picture, but this time it was one of him and his prison homies. I felt proud to show off that I had an older brother who cared enough to write to me even in difficult times.

As for José, when he got released, he got deported. Later, he somehow crossed the border illegally, and when he was in the United States he made sure to stop by my house to say hi before driving to Oxnard. I saw him six years after, but throughout that time he kept in contact with me. He called me when he was drunk and oftentimes mistook me for one of his girlfriends.

Eventually, both of my brothers were deported and ended up in Tijuana. When Carlos was released from prison, he went directly to TJ. José ended up self-deporting himself because he started to mess up again and everyone in the family advised him to go with Carlos before the cops arrested him. Although it was hard for them to live in Mexico, away from their family, it was also hard for me because once again our chain had been broken, and the little hope I had of being closer had vanished. Now a border wall divided us even more than before.

We see each other once a year, because in my situation, it is difficult for me to cross into TJ because the roads are too chaotic for me to push my wheelchair around; but when I do go, I make sure to let my brothers know that I love them despite the fact that we aren't as close as I wish we could be. I want to create memories with them, because the only times I've been around them, I can count with my ten fingers. Now, I make sure we take a picture together so that our memories can last like the one Polaroid picture that I have up on my living room wall of my dad and brothers.

María Morales is a mother of five children who spent more than 15 years fighting a war with drugs and the stigma that comes with it. As a woman who was personally caught up in the judicial system, María has made it her number-one goal to use her experience by sharing her story with others as a way to connect and make change.

María Morales
"I" Am Home

To my superhero and best friend, my DAD.

I remember I could feel the sticky humidity on the back of my neck on that hot September evening when I came across something out of the ordinary. I was taking a stroll through downtown San Diego when I saw a young lady holding a baby in her arms sitting on the front steps of an apartment complex with two little girls at her side. Maybe it was my empathetic heart that pulled me to the tears that this young lady was wiping from her cheeks, or the fear that I saw as she attempted to soothe the two little girls. I can still see the confusion that molded their faces, as they couldn't have been more than three and four years old. I wanted to reach out and envelop them in my arms, yet something stopped me as I watched this scene continue before my eyes. Then suddenly the young lady stood up with a renewed look of strength on her face and put whatever she could fit along with the baby into the stroller. I heard her speak the names "Angelica" and "Maricella" as she softly told them to stay right next to her as they began to walk down the street. I didn't know where they were going or the story they shared but I knew I could not leave them alone.

I sit on the front steps of the apartment complex. I have just been shoved out into the silence of a city, and I am lost. Surrounding me are my worldly possessions, my two little daughters and my newborn son, Eugene. What just happened? Where is my dad? I can feel the tears running down my cheeks but I must hold them back because these two sets of big brown eyes are looking at me in confusion. They are depending on me to keep them safe. Yet, how can I keep them safe when obviously I cannot keep myself safe? I have to find some strength so I pack as much as I can into the stroller, whisper to my girls to stay right next to me and we start walking. I have no idea where we are walking but I know we have to go somewhere. I need a home. I need my dad.

Somehow I found myself like an angel in this family's wake. My soul longed to help and to give them what they needed, yet all I could do was watch from a distance. I could see the lost look in their eyes as they stood in the shadows of the streets of downtown San Diego. Where was their home? Was there no one to help them? I screamed inside wanting them to hear my pleas, "I am here with you, you are not alone." Then suddenly a car pulled up to the family, and the man inside called the young lady. She slowly walked to the car with her head down with what looked like shame. After a short conversation, a young man got out of the car and talked to her family. He then proceeded to help them load their stuff into his car, and they all got in and they drove away.

I remember our first night so clearly, homeless and desperate on the streets. We finally find my dad returning from an AA meeting and I tell him what happened. I need him to tell me everything is going to be okay, that someone will help us but he has no answers. The evening turns into night and we just walk until we find ourselves standing under a storefront, hiding in the shadows. I want no one to see me with three little children and no place to go. I suddenly notice a car driving back and forth watching us. As my shame deepens, it finally pulls over and stops. A man calls me over to his car and I don't know what to expect but maybe this is help? I am so desperate at this moment. I remember him asking if my kids and I are okay and if we need help. I tell him our story, that we had nowhere to go. So he gets out of his car, speaks to my dad and offers us help. I feel such relief when he says he wants to pay for a night at the hotel where my dad's car had broken down. We then pile into this kind man's car and head towards a fate unknown.

The next night, this beautiful family quieted for the night inside a lone car that looked to be abandoned in the parking lot at the back of a motel. I felt so many intense emotions emanate from the car—excitement from Angelica and Maricella, helplessness from the young lady's father and utter fear and terror from her. What had happened to this family that could bring such immense feelings that overpowered the joys of life? The night got quiet as they began to rest.

My shame lurks in the shadows as the night quiets. As my two little angels have their camping adventure in the back seat, my dad sleeps in the driver's side, my newborn snuggles in the middle and I am in the front passenger seat covering the windows with towels, thinking, "If I can't see them, they can't see me." I pray no one would see us sleeping in the broken-down car in the parking lot of the Goodnite Inn in Chula Vista. Would they notice us, the family with no destination? Is this our home? The night slowly turns into day....

It had been a long night for the family, and I sensed the feeling of hopelessness as the front door opened and the young lady's dad got out of the car. What had caused all this deep sorrow that lingered in their wake? I felt helpless, because I wanted them to know it would all be okay and that they needed to stay strong. I imagined my arms around them and knew my faith would bring light to their day.

As the sun rises, I can sense that my dad is leaving the car with his used McDonald's coffee cup. I know that's where he finds sanctuary, with a cup of coffee and the morning newspaper. It's where he hides from the reality of our world. My dad comes back revived after having his hour of rest before the kids wake up. He encourages my daughters to go have breakfast with him at "the restaurant" which is in fact St. Vincent de Paul's free meal program for the homeless. I am too prideful, so I stay in the car. I feed my baby and clean up for a day that will be filled with walking the streets of San Diego. There will be hours spent at the welfare office, begging for any kind of help they can assist us with and at the

WIC office, to see if we can get anything extra. It will be the beginning of many mornings of tears flowing over dried WIC cereal for me.

Days were turning into weeks, and I was now fearful that no one would help "my family." I have walked with them as they struggled to grasp at any hope. It felt like many days of walking with no destination. You could see the exhaustion in their walk and the weariness in the smiles that had become less and less frequent. Angelica and Maricella seemed to be holding up a lot better than their mom and grandpa. They seemed to be the only reason the family continued to push forward. "Please don't give up," I whispered in their ears as they slept, and wished them pleasant dreams as they attempted to rest their souls. Tomorrow would be another day....

Our days have now turned into little field trips to Seaport Village. Our food stamps are our only resource, but they provide us food for our picnics—watching the pelican with a broken wing and enjoying the beautiful views of the San Diego bay. As our days slowly come to an end, and after the kids have bathed in the motel pool, they climb back into the car to rest. This is the time I attempt to find a payphone, any payphone that will allow me to make a collect call. These are the moments I break. I plead and beg my mom to please let us come home. Desperation fills my cries, and anger rolls down my cheeks disguised as tears. It always ends with me screaming, "Please, Mom, please let us come home," and all I hear is the dial tone at the other end of the line. My world comes swirling to an end at that moment. Emptiness fills my heart. I'll try again tomorrow.

"Why? Why? Why?" raced through my mind as I witnessed this pain and I shed a tear.

Minutes have turned into hours; hours are turning into days; and days have turned into nights. It has taken weeks for us to be saved but the moment is fast approaching, I feel it. It's another night of me covering the windows, hiding our shame, when I hear the sound I have feared but also longed for. I hear the knock on my window and I open my door.

There are three cop cars and one too many police around the car. They let us know that they had a call about a family living in a car in the motel parking lot. We explain our situation and they ask us to come down to the police station with them. They tell me if I cannot find a safe place for my children that they will have to notify the Department of Social Services and have my children removed from my care. But all I hear is that I am "an unfit mother who does not deserve her children" in their voices. My heart is racing and all I know is that I can't lose my babies. I have to find a safe place for them. I call everyone but no one can help until finally someone stands up for me. I never knew what that felt like until this moment. The sergeant of the Chula Vista police department calls my mother back after her initial "no, this-is-not-my-problem" response and tells her that she has a responsibility to take my children and me in. Someone believes in me and feels I deserve to be helped. They then take us to have dinner at Denny's and get us a hotel room. I sleep like an angel that night, my soul at peace.

Relief! That was way too close. My little family would finally be going home. I saw hope in Maria's eyes but there was still a deeper sadness lingering in her heart. Why was she still so sad? They were saved last night. Shouldn't she be filled with happiness and not those unshed, lingering tears that I felt and saw? I didn't understand.

We are going home today, back to Indio. But the "we" does not include my dad. I have such a broken heart as we wait for a police officer to pick us up from the hotel. They will be dropping us off at St. Vincent de Paul's to apply for free Greyhound bus tickets for my children and me. It's going to be a long day of just waiting.

"What?" I didn't understand. Why was her dad being left behind? Where would he go? What would happen to him?

As the Greyhound pulls up and we get ready to board, my heart struggles to allow me on the bus. How can I leave my dad on the streets all by himself? What will happen to him? But my dad promises me he will be okay and that I need to take care of my children. How can he be so strong? Isn't he scared? My dad is my world and I feel like I am abandoning him. He urges me to get on the bus and I hug him tightly, not knowing what will happen to him. As the bus begins to pull away, all I can do is wave goodbye. Tears stream down my cheeks. I am unable to find the strength to hold them in any longer.

As the bus heads forward and my heart searches for a way to calm as my children and I head towards safety, a lady sits across from us on the bus. She smiles at me and for some reason I feel a wave of love ease my heart. Then, softly, I hear a voice telling me, *"I have been with you, through every tear you have shed, through all the anger and disappointments, the fears and loneliness you have felt, and now, as your heart is heavy, I am with you. I will be with you until you learn to find your voice. I will not abandon or give up on you. I will teach you that you are worth more than you believe. I will fight for you and envelop you with love when you feel you do not deserve to be loved. I will be your strength when you feel like you will fall, and I will be that step that takes you further. My name is María Elena and I will hold your hand as we walk through life together. You are not alone. I am your home."*

Photo: Sarah Loud

Ryan "Flaco" Rising is now a student leader at San Diego City College with a vision to end recidivism and to build the prison-to-school pipeline. Formerly incarcerated, Flaco is using his experience to help inspire change and reduce the mass incarceration epidemic that's destroying so many communities in our country. He believes that it is up to us, together as one, to create change in our community.

Thanks for your support!

Ryan Rising

Ryan "Flaco" Rising
Second Chances

I dedicate this story to the people of San Diego and I sincerely
apologize for everything I did that hurt this community.

I have lived a life full of second chances. When I really break it down, I'm lucky to be alive. My first second chance was given to me at the age of five, when I was an adventurous young boy who was exploring the world and everything in it. I was in a Jacuzzi in the apartment where my babysitter lived and was wondering why the drain had such an intense suction power. In my imagination, I thought it was a warp zone. So, I dove down to explore by lifting up the plate that covered it. I stuck my arm in, and it grabbed onto my arm like a vacuum. It felt like a monster had me by the arm and wouldn't let go. I tried anything and everything to get out, but I was stuck! I held my breath and don't remember much else after that. I was pronounced dead on the scene after they pulled me out and unsuccessfully gave me CPR. They got me into the ambulance and gave my heart an electric shock and that gave me a pulse. They then Life Flighted me to Children's Hospital which specialized in drowning, and put me into a coma. I like to think that while I was in that trance state, I was in a deep discussion with my maker. We looked at my future life and decided that it was important for me to live. He sent me back on a mission. Honestly, I truly believe that I'm here for a reason.

Life after that day hasn't been easy. I struggled all the way through school. I was told I had ADHD. They gave me all types of different medication that made me explode in class, become suicidal, and ultimately not fit in with my peers. They put me in the resource room with the kids who were severely handicapped and secluded me from the regular classroom. This was my experience with school. This treatment had a huge psychological effect on me. It drove me to act out in ways I probably never would have if I had been treated normally. So there I was, a teenager who had been suspended all the way through elementary school. I even got paddled by my principal in the fourth grade for exploding in class. As an out-of-control, misunderstood kid, I felt lonely. Nobody understood me. This was my upbringing. I was constantly fighting and was a bully towards other kids. I ended up in juvenile hall where I would continue to act out and explode. I would fight and be isolated from everyone else.

My next second chance came while I was in a juvenile work ranch. At 13 years old, I was in a lodge that housed about 25 kids, and two of the older kids were about to turn 18. I hated being there. It sucked. We bucked 50-pound bales of hay all day long (stacked them on the truck). We used pitchforks to clean horse stalls, and they kept us constantly busy working and cleaning horses. So, these two older kids were thinking that since they hadn't completed the program, they were going to be shipped to the detention center or moved into the prison system. They were panicking and decided to go on the run, so I joined them.

We went on a wild crime spree: robbed stores, stole a bunch of guns, and ultimately ended up in Oregon. There we got into a high-speed chase with the highway patrol, ended up slamming into a fence, and I went through the front windshield. I remember waking up, standing, trying to run and hearing, "Get the fuck down motherfucker or else I will shoot." So I froze and fell to the ground, only to hear three gunshots ring out—boom, boom, boom. I was thinking in my head, "He shot me!" I looked for blood, but didn't see any. Then, I realized it was the other two kids who had tried to shoot at the cops. Why the police didn't shoot back, I don't know, but here I am, at 13 years old, looking at a life sentence for attempted murder of a police officer and all types of felonies, in a holding tank in some honky-tonk town in Oregon. Not knowing what my future holds, I sit there in a jail cell for two weeks. Then one day, they open my door and say transportation is here for me. I'm going back to the youth ranch. They cuff me up and I get into a prison van with bars, by myself, only to find out that the district attorney in Oregon picked up all the charges on the other two. Since I'm thirteen, they can't charge me as an adult, so they just drop the charges on me and send me to Idaho where they charge me as a juvenile on fifteen counts of grand theft. I'm sentenced and have to stay at the work ranch for another six or seven months. Then, they send me back to the detention center where I'm locked up for what seemed to me a very long time. And then one day, they come over to me and just say, "You're out of here."

Next thing I know, I was 16 and on a plane heading to see my mother. After years of being confined, this was a huge culture shock. My mom lived in a small, boring town in Montana, and I was a California gang member who dressed way differently than everyone else. So, right away, I was tested and had to fight to earn my respect. I soon became the local town drug connection. Just like that, I was back into the game. My reputation got me kicked out of high school and had me under countless investigations. It was rough, but hold up—this is about second chances. So, back to my final second chance.

Honestly, I don't know how I've gotten so many second chances in this life, but I have. And so at that point, I was in my twenties, selling and using drugs and really out of control. I am constantly moving around and have no type of direction in my life. I am lost. I first lose my high school sweetheart, and then the mother of my daughter. So I have this fuck-the-world attitude. I get back into my gangster mentality and I am back to robbing. So I am out here in San Diego, out of control, running up on people with a gun, taking their hard-earned money to support my crystal meth habit. Then it all comes to a screeching halt. I have a split second to think, what do I do? I am in my car, pulled over by the police; I have a gun and all types of stolen goods. So I get out and lock my car and start to walk away, only to be asked back into my car by the officer. This was the end of a long run.

I am in a jail cell facing car jacking, bank robbery, possession of a firearm and a gang enhancement. On all of it, I'm looking at a life sentence, but the FBI drops the bank robbery on me—lack of evidence. They offer me a deal of twelve years. I tell them, "No. Let's go for a fast and speedy trial." By the next court date, they come back with six years with 85%, meaning I get fifteen percent good time, but I would have to sign the deal that day. I sign it and find myself on the Grey Goose, headed to Donovan from George Bailey. I've never been in prison so I don't know what's ahead in this new journey. I am asked to identify my ethnicity. I tell them I am Mexican and they look at me like I'm crazy. This isn't the first time I'm looked at like this, so I'm used to it. You see, this has happened to me my whole life. I am a Mexican with blond hair, blue eyes, and white skin. I'm sure you're wondering how that happened. My dad is Mexican and my mom is white. There is a story behind it, but I will explain it one day when I'm ready to deal with it. But this prison guard can't believe me so he says, "Okay, you Whitexican. Good luck with them South Siders. You will be stabbed and killed in a week." I look at him, undeterred, and go to my holding tank.

This journey was full of brutal, disgusting treatment. I experienced the utmost filthy conditions. They fed me the most revolting meals, and I had to deal with the worst segregation I've ever seen in my life. Two months after I was in prison, my first son was born. So, now what? I have a son and a daughter and I am in prison. I feel like shit. Can't believe this is where I put myself, but I keep pushing. Then, the worst thing ever, the mother of my children, who has been writing, promising me my dream, which is to have my family and raise my children with her as my wife, meets another man and gets married. I am broken. My mom is okay with it and tells me to get over it, but inside, I feel betrayed and so alone. My dream is broken.

They ask me for a favor on the yard. One of our homeys is snitching to the institutional gang unit. They got it on paper. I'm feeling at this point, this is my life, so I say yes. Next yard, they tell me who he is, and I am shown my crimees, the guys who will go with me, and I am handed a knife. I go over to where the snitch is working out. He has no clue and as he jumps down off the pull-up bar, I, along with my homeys, start to stab him. We pass off our homemade knives and start to kick while he is down on the floor. We jump on his head and then I am shot two times by the block gun. I am sprayed with pepper spray that drops me to the floor. They Life Flight the snitch off the yard. This changes my whole entire reputation in prison. I turn into a legend, "That's Flaco, the one who stabbed the snitch." I go to the back, which is officially called the segregated housing unit. This is where I learned how to be a disciplined soldier. We are up at five in the morning and we have to listen to our name on the tier and yell loud and proud, "Buenos días. Buenos días." Then we all work out together in the cages. Everything in the workout routine is done together. We yell with pride like a military infantry group. I went through that for 15 months.

Then, one day, they cuffed me up and said I was going back to the main line. They transferred me to a level-four maximum security prison called Salinas Valley, better known as the "death octagon," since so many inmates die or are killed there. I learned quickly that this is a vicious place. The first yard I go to, I see a homey get his neck split with a shank. "*YARD RECALL!*" They leave us on lockdown for a couple of months; then, they bring us up off lockdown and it would happen again. Another stabbing. Another long lockdown. This is how my time in Salinas Valley went. Then we started programming (going to the yard and going to school) and out of nowhere, a vicious prison riot erupts. We, the Sureños, against the Norteños (Southern California Mexicans and the Northern California Mexicans). They rushed us with a bunch of homemade knives, but we outnumbered them by 25 and we savagely protected ourselves. This was my first experience with a riot. They are the bloodiest barbarian events; it's very hard to explain to a person who has never been through it. Right after this, I was transferred to New Folsom.

Two months later I got my next second chance. I was out at the yard, walking with a homey around the track. I'll never forget this moment: a bird took a shit on his shirt. I started clowning him. "Haha, Ese, you got shitted on by a bird." We continued around the track over to a water fountain so the homey could wash his shirt, not knowing that a bloody riot, one of the most gruesome in New Folsom's State Prison's history, was about to erupt. I remember it got very quiet, and then homey looked up at me and said, "Is it me or did it just get super-quiet?" I looked over to see a couple homeys digging up our stash of butcher knives. I then saw all the homeys gathered up at the top of the hill on our property. I told the homey, "Let's get to our property. Somethin's up." We get up there and the homey hands me a huge butcher knife, looks me in the eyes and says, "We're rushing the Bay Area Blacks," and within the blink of an eye we were like army ants rushing at full speed. As the Bay Area Blacks came running towards us, I started to stab and stick a guy and it all became a blur. I was screaming, "SUR TRECE," at the top of my lungs as I stabbed a guy who fell to the ground. And then I heard, "SSSSSS," and concrete chunks hit me in the face. I repositioned myself as I continued to stab this guy on the floor. I was full of warrior adrenaline that I didn't know existed in me. And again, "SSSSS. BOOM!" Concrete chunks hit me again. I looked over at the wall to see two huge chunks of the wall missing. I saw a prison officer zeroing in on me with a mini-14 semiautomatic rifle pointed at my head. I then realized he was trying to kill me. I instantly stopped, then took off running up a hill to see a group of my homeys getting three Bay Areas. We were shot at again. By the time this battle ended, it had gone on for ten minutes. When I sat down and came back to my mind, I saw bloody bodies laying everywhere. As I watched them escort lifeless bodies off the yard and looked around to see all of my homeys on top of the hill in the Bay Areas' property, it dawned on me that I almost got shot in the head, twice. We sat there for hours as helicopters flew around in the air. It was all over the news. We were on lockdown for almost two years after this riot.

During this lockdown they offered us college courses and I started to study at Lassen Community College. We didn't meet with a teacher; they would give us the books through the door and we would send everything in through the mail. I started to study. This was a turning point in my life. I realized that I needed to use this second chance and quit living life on the edge. I had two kids and I needed to work on a better legacy, so I studied hard and read self-help books. I really became dedicated to building my mind and maturing as a man. Finally, I created my goals and started to dream again. For the first time ever, I really began to envision a better life.

Four years after that life I got a second chance in society. The gates opened up and I walked out of the vicious war zone and back to civilian life. I am super-relieved that I made it out of the devil's playground alive. I began this new journey in my life with a humble heart. I have my heart set to do the right things. I am in college and I am working towards my associate degree. I am staying very focused and loyal to my goals. I honestly believe I am here for a great reason, and all these second chances prove that. I have a great future ahead of me and I now honestly realize that *I* am the writer of this script called life. So as I pursue my dreams and look towards becoming successful, I feel real good about everything I am doing. I don't let any of the negatives or challenges I face every day sidetrack me or get me down. Because, honestly, I will never forget where I came from. This is my second chance and I refuse to fail. I will make the best out of this and leave behind a legacy my friends and family will share forever.

Thanks for this second chance. I am truly grateful and blessed to be here sharing this story with you.

Monique Sandoval is a Barrio Logan resident. She's currently a San Diego City College student majoring in communication and radio television with an emphasis on Chicana/o Studies. She's an activist on and off campus in clubs like MEChA and Pillars of the Community Scholars Society, in hopes to make this world a better place for the next generation.

Monique Sandoval
Robbed

*I dedicate this piece to my brothers who were the inspiration to my
story, and the rest of my family, but also to those who've been there
every step of the way of my writing process.*

Logan Heights, an area people call ghetto, rough, and dangerous, will
for me always be home. It's a place where all the neighbors, from across
the street to down the block, knew each other. A place where all the
neighborhood kids would come out to play football or baseball on Evans
Street until the sun went down. I can still hear the echo of my childhood
when I walk down that old street of mine, recalling how someone would
scream, "CAR!" and every single kid would run to different corners of
the sidewalk as that car interrupted our game. Everyone would watch for
a second as it drove away then run back to continue the game. I remember those hot summer days when we had water balloon and water gun
fights. I remember walking down to the Barrio Station swimming pool
with towels in hand. It was the place I formed many close relationships.

I still reside in Logan Heights, where I am constantly reminded that
the neighborhood I have grown up in is known primarily for its dark
side. Part of the dark side is the gangs and cliques in the area (Logan
Heights Red Steps, 30th Street, Barrio Sherman, and Shelltown) that are
constantly after each other for a piece of street cred. And then there's the
infinite amount of tagging and graffiti on the walls. I never looked at the
writing on the walls as vandalism; rather, I looked at it as an expression
of art, especially since I lived across the street from Chicano Park which
has become known for the famous artwork on the pillars. I soon noticed

how clean walls would appear as a canvas for the gangs in the area on Chicano Park Day. The gangs would tag them up as way of honoring their hood on this historical day—the day that the community took over this little piece of land and still gathers in celebration every year to ensure our tradition stays alive with the youth.

In time, I began to notice that the dark side my neighborhood was known for made me feel like people were looking down on me when I would hear remarks like, "Oh, you're from *there*," or the questions, "Aren't you afraid to walk around there?" when I told people where I was from. Yes, the neighborhood has been portrayed on the news as a violent gang territory, and yes, I sort of grew up around the gang lifestyle, but I never felt that it affected my life as a child until I got older and became aware of the situations I witnessed. The repeated scenes of violence are like a bad soundtrack of the corrupt system that has robbed my brothers and me in so many ways. I have nine brothers, yet I only got to know a few of them. The dark side took them away from me and kept them caught up in a constant cycle of prison, street life and poverty.

The dark side to my neighborhood was not just the gang life, it was also the constant police hostility and harassment. As a young child I never saw the cops as the bad guys. I remember for years around Christmastime police officers and fire fighters would pass out toys, stickers and fake badges to the kids in the neighborhood. I remember watching them on TV and hearing the song, "Bad boys, bad boys, what you gonna do? What you gonna do when they come for you?" That song would paint a vivid image for me that the cops were the good guys out to arrest the bad guys, but I would soon learn that wasn't always the truth.

I was eight years old when I first observed the police's negative impact in my community. It was late in the evening and my older brothers Jaime and Mario sat outside with their friend Benjamin making jokes and listening to music. The sound of their deep laughter permeated the front door while my mother, youngest sister and I watched TV in the living room. The front door opened as my brothers Jaime and Mario came into the house. A few moments later there was an unrecognizable heavy knock at the door; my mother got up from the sofa to open it. There stood two gentlemen at our doorway dressed all in black from top to bottom. I turned and looked at my sister and said, "COPS!" I was overwhelmed by a sense of confusion and fear, not understanding why these feelings stirred within me until I heard them ask if anyone by the name of "Jaime" lived in our home. My mother answered yes and then proceeded to ask how she could help them. "Ma'am, would you do us a favor and call him out?" My mother replied, "Can I know what this is in regards to?" "We received a call that your son was in a physical altercation with a young man a few houses down." My mother, confused, responded, "Officers, my sons have been home the whole time and they've never left the yard." She then called out for my brother, "Jaime, come out." Jaime stepped out of the room as my sister and I sat on the sofa looking at the cops standing on our porch under that dim light of ours while our mother stood in the doorway.

Next thing I knew, two officers placed my brother in handcuffs for his very first time without asking a single question. I was just a kid standing next to her sobbing mother witnessing her big brother being arrested, trying to understand what was going on. I was an eight-year-old girl, looking at the guys I had always seen as the good guys taking away my brother—a good guy himself. I wasn't really sure what I should've been feeling when I saw the cuffs fastened on my brother's wrists, but I started to question. Was he the bad guy? He was the brother who brushed my hair and put it into a braid, a ponytail, or pigtails for me on school days, the brother who helped me with my homework and who would babysit all the kids when the grown-ups would go out. As he walked over to the cop car with the men in uniform, I felt tears welling up in my eyes from the fear that I would not see my brother again. I wanted to scream at them to let him go, but I didn't. I don't know what stopped me; maybe it was seeing my mom cry or holding my little sister's hand as we watched it all happen. I wasn't aware at that moment that my family would be robbed that day. And unfortunately, it wouldn't be the last time I would witness one of my brothers placed in handcuffs.

The altercation my brother was arrested for was nothing but a misunderstanding. Benjamin was my brother Mario's friend who lived one house down from our sky blue house. The boys had been messing around earlier that day and Jaime threw a toy wrestler figure at Benjamin. It hit his ear and he went home that evening upset that his ear had been cut by the toy action figure. His grandmother wasn't aware of how it had happened so she called the cops assuming that Benjamin had been intentionally harmed. My brother Jaime was placed into the back of the cop car for throwing a toy at someone.

Benjamin admitted it had been an accident, that they were just goofing around and he had thrown the toy first. Benjamin's mother and grandmother didn't want to press charges and they begged the officer to let my brother go, but the officer, unmoved, said, "It's a little too late for you to say you don't want to press charges." See, three years before this incident, when he was 15 years old, Jaime had gotten into a fight coming home from San Diego High School with another student. They both fled the scene and neither of them suffered serious injuries. Despite this, the family of the kid he fought wanted to press charges and there had been a warrant out for his arrest since then. When pulling up his information in response to this action figure accident, the police officers found that he had a warrant out for the fight he was in when he was 15. Jaime was 18 now, so he was legally an adult in the eyes of the State of California and was going to be charged for something he had done when he was 15 years old.

Jaime was the first brother to be taken away to jail in front of me and I remember sobbing my eyes out next to my mother as the cop car drove away down that dark street on Evans. I was too young to understand what had just happened.

My brother Jaime wrote letters to my mom, my sister and me. My sister and I always tried to write to him as often as we could because we would look forward to hearing from him about how long he had left, and the things we would do when he returned home. We knew that these letters were a sign of hope for him to stay out of trouble and to make time pass quickly.

My brother Jamie would never be the same. After serving six months for his first offense, he came out a different man. Who would have thought that a teen scuffle would end up propelling my brother into the system and forever change the trajectory of his life? He would end up back in prison over and over again, unable to break the cycle that had taken hold of him. We would never get to do the things he had promised us when I was a kid.

At the age of nine I witnessed yet another incident of police harassment. I thought I was having a dream: Cops with guns and flashlights pointed at me and my younger sister stormed in as we laid in our bunk beds. The police ordered us to get out of our beds and walk into the living room where my mom, brother Mario, and my brother Juan's wife sat. It wasn't a dream. I remember looking at the black cable box with the red numbers reading the time, 4:45 a.m. I thought to myself it was way too early in the morning for us to be up. We still had a couple of hours before school started. It was freezing and the cold breeze entered from our front door which was left wide open by the police, granting me a view of my older brothers Jaime and Juan who were outside in little clothing in the early morning, freezing cold. Bright lights flashed, because photos were taken of my brothers' faces and one of my brothers' tattoos. They were trying to associate him with a gang by identifying his tattoos.

My sister-in-law, who was sitting next to us on the sofa, was rocking my two-month-old baby nephew who was fast asleep in his blue onesie despite all the noise of the walkie-talkies and cops coming in and out of the house.

I wasn't sure what had happened or why they were there, but we had heard rumors that some of our neighbors had been raided during the weeks leading up to our very own encounter. Around that time, the police seemed to routinely raid homes in my area every so often in the summer. Anyone who fit the description of a gang member would get their picture taken and anyone with an outstanding warrant would get arrested. After taking pictures, leaving them handcuffed for a while, and checking their records, they let Juan and Jaime go, but they arrested my brother Ramón.

We were all robbed yet again, in one way or another, that day. Ramón, who was 17 at the time, would be robbed of his freedom by the city that would force him to sign a plea deal and confess to a crime he didn't commit because my mother couldn't afford to offer him a good defense lawyer. He would be robbed of growing up to be a young man the proper way, but we both would be robbed from getting to know each other, because by the time Ramón would be released, I would be in my junior year of high school and not that dorky little nine-year-old girl when he left.

Ramón hardly ever called or wrote to us while he was gone. He said it was too hard for him to hear our voices. We never went to see Ramón because they transferred him so far from home to so many different places—including the Southern Youth Reception Center in Norwalk; the Preston School of Industry, a reform school in Ione, California; Heman G. Stark Youth Correctional Facility in Chino; the California Correctional Institution in Tehachapi; and finally, the California State Prison, Corcoran, where he would serve out the rest of his time until coming back home. From this list you can see that he graduated from juvenile detention to maximum-security prisons.

My next experience with the dark side of law enforcement would come on my 20th birthday, a day that is supposed to be an enjoyable day for many, but not for me. Unlike many others whose birthday memories are full of warm, loving memories, mine would be peppered with anger and fear. On the day of my birthday, my immediate family all came over for the usual birthday celebration dinner. My mom had put a feast together of my favorite foods: nachos, hot wings, enchiladas, rice and beans. One by one, my siblings started to arrive with their families or spouses. My brothers Fernando and Juan came with their families, my sisters with theirs. My brother Mario had to work so his little family came, and then, of course, the family-in-laws came too. My brother Jaime surprised me by coming down from Escondido with a counselor from Amity Vista Ranch, a rehabilitation program that he entered as yet another deal with the state. Jaime came to join in the festivities with us, so we all got together and took a family photo. As we finished taking our photo, we all stood outside and gathered in the yard making jokes. My brother Jaime stood outside the yard to smoke a cigarette away from the kids and my mom, who was diagnosed with emphysema. As my brother and his counselor stood outside the gate, a cop car drove by slowly, pulled over and parked in the middle of the street and the officer asked what was going on. Then he proceeded to get out of the car, and right then another cop car passed by, made a u-turn, and also stopped in front of our home. The officers got out of their cars, walked towards us and started harassing my brother Jaime. Jaime and his counselor were placed in handcuffs for no good reason other than the cop had recognized my brother. They searched them while the rest of us were ordered to stay in the yard. We all had to sit there and watch the horrifying yet familiar scene play out again. Yet again, the dark side robbed us of our time together and humiliated my brother, who had done nothing illegal.

As I got older, it became harder to form a relationship with my brothers; it hasn't been an easy road. It's a work in progress because they were absent so much of the time I wanted or needed them to be around. For a very long time I have held my brothers to blame for robbing us of having a relationship because they fell into that lifestyle and weren't able to get out. We missed out on growing up together. I was free compared to them because I was able to do what I wanted for the most part, while they were stuck growing up in chains and working for nine cents an hour. Eventually, my brothers would come home though we were practically strangers. They would try to build a relationship between us but would soon give up because we could not see eye to eye. I never knew how to talk to them about what they actually went through while incarcerated nor did they know how to talk to me about my life without them. All I knew was that I did not want to be another addition to that cycle or seen by my family as a failure by following the same patterns. I wanted to make a better future for myself and for my mom who always seemed to support everyone despite it all. I was the first person to graduate from high school and to further my education by attending college where I have become aware of the effects of the prison industrial system on families and communities. My story is one of the many stories of a family that has been robbed by the system. I wanted to share with you the beauty of my barrio, the infamous "Barrio Logan," through my eyes and through the eyes of the system that has criminalized us because of where we live. I share with you the stories of our brothers that we tend to lose and never really get back, from a sister's point of view, as I fight hard to reclaim my life and my relationships with my brothers.

Photo: Sarah Loud

Dawood Shabazz was born and raised in San Diego. His mother was
a telephone operator, and his father was a drug dealer from Chicago. When
he was three years old, his father went to prison for a drug-related incident,
leaving his single mother alone to raise Dawood and his brother and sister.
After his mother's violent death, which Dawood witnessed, the children
were raised by an aunt. Dawood loved basketball, and was an active and
popular kid, but in his mid-teens, he was introduced to drugs and alcohol,
which he used to suppress his depression and anxieties. After graduating
high school, his plan was to be a hustler, selling bootleg movies, CDs, and
even legal services. Now, he is pursuing a dream of becoming a successful
entrepreneur/businessman.

Dawood Shabazz
The Night My Mother Was Murdered

*I dedicate my story to my black queen mother, Belinda Gail
Matory, who is my constant inspiration, my source of guilt and
beloved driving force, and equally to my brothers and soldiers in the
struggle.*

It was the night before Halloween, better yet, the morning before, as
it had to be around two o'clock in the morning. My younger brother,
older sister and I had just concluded watching Halloween movies before
falling fast asleep in our beds. I even remember dreaming about Tim
Burton's *Nightmare Before Christmas* that night. To this day, that movie
lingers pessimistically in my consciousness. Suddenly we were awoken
by screams and banging in the house. It turned out to be my mother and
her boyfriend arguing and fighting. The first thing I witnessed as I awoke
was a large gash in the wall as my mother ran panicking into the room
to gather us because we had to leave. We were to go to our godmother's
house as it had been planned.

At that young age we didn't comprehend fully what was going on
until our mother explained to us in the car. We were getting away from
"that man" and everything was going to be all right, especially because we
were able to bring our costumes with us for trick or treating that night.
My mom was a single mother to the three of us. Our sister had a different
father and he was in prison. My father was also in prison. Even at that
age, my mother noticeably and constantly searched for love. Her newest
boyfriend lived with us, which was a new condition that we weren't used
to, but we didn't mind because at that time we had grown fond of him,

although deep inside I still longed for my father. I remember my mother once asking us for our approval of him, and we wanted him to be our temporary daddy—until this night when we ran from him.

We had cut a few corners around the block in my mother's vehicle that read "PBW" for Proud Black Woman on the license plate, and then she made a sudden stop. That moment I remember a vague conversation in which she told me I would one day be successful.

My mother told us to stay in the car as she got out and walked towards a white house. It was dark and spooky. The next thing I know we witnessed our mother running from a man into the street. We heard screams and then gunshots as she hit the ground. Her shooter ended up on top of her. That's when I got out of the car and yelled, "Get off my mommy!" I remember striking him in the head. My brother and sister stayed by the car. The man then got off of my mother as she lay bleeding profusely in the street. He glanced at me and I will never forget his deranged look as he laughed, turned the gun on himself and blew his brains out.

We were all shocked, crying as two people—one whom we loved dearly—lay in the street, lifeless. It was the first time I saw dead bodies; the feeling was unreal. It felt like a living nightmare when I tried to nudge my mother back to life. In my dismay, I even tried to open her eyelids. My brother and sister were at a distance, but I was all too close. I screamed to them that this had to be a dream. I told them we would wake up soon. My mother died in her nightgown on some street in Spring Valley. I have yet to experience a more emotionally numbing and depressed state of utter helplessness as I felt the night my mother was murdered in front of my eyes.

The Aftermath

I am a firm believer that no one can love you like your mother. There is no love more sincere than a mother's affection, and it definitely molds an individual into his or her adulthood. The feeling of being needed or even wanted comes from being a mother's baby. When my mother died, my siblings and I never got the same type of affection from our aunt and uncle. My aunt, my mother's older sister, took us in to live with her husband and their two kids who were both older than us by a few years. My aunt thought that it was best for us to stay with the family rather than go with our godmother with whom my mother had willed for us to go if anything happened to her. Being raised by my aunt and uncle was pretty tough at times. As a young boy I depended on my mother exclusively. She was my support, my comfort. With her gone I felt like I was alone. Not only that but I felt that nobody else was qualified to tell me what to do, and under our new military-like guardianship, that attitude led to conflict. I remember my mother's death being announced to everyone at my school at Johnson Elementary. I remember the kids telling me everything was okay and the elders consoling me. Prior to her death, in my second grade class I was the popular kid. I was very outgoing, outspoken and well liked. When my mother passed, I remember there being a shift in my attitude. I now grew withdrawn and even embarrassed. I felt awkward knowing that people knew about my situation. I felt sort of crippled, motherless in a room full of kids with mothers. Not having a father in my school for us black kids unfortunately wasn't so uncommon. But now I didn't have a mother or father! I felt like kids were laughing at me behind my back, and I was ready to fight at a pin drop. If I heard anyone talking about their mother, positively or negatively, it made my heart twitch. I wasn't the same. I later learned that setting myself apart from everybody—outcasting myself—might have been the defining moment that solidified my personality up until this day. It's the feeling that nobody here is like me or feels what I feel, or has seen what I've seen.

The affection stripped from me at the age of seven defines now how I relate to the rest of the world. I was now different and everybody knew it. I grew overly sensitive at heart. My relationships up until recently, including a marriage that ended in divorce, would be unstable and I believe the foundation of my emotional problems stem psychologically from this incident. When you witness violence at a helpless age, once you come into strength, you tend to replicate it. I became inflamed with aggression as a child and I would take my anger out on my brother as well as on my classmates. My emotions have the ability to alter almost instantly and I hate feeling weak; therefore, to act as the aggressor was preferred all the way into my adulthood. I have a deep drive that when stimulated can turn me into a beast of an athlete or just a beast. I live with a constant chip on my shoulder and no one to run to but myself.

I remember throughout my childhood actually fantasizing about having a mother and father and showing them off in front of other kids. While others would complain about their biological relationships, I would imagine them. There is no love like a mother's love.

The effects of violence linger in an individual and acts as either an emotional suppressor or an adrenaline. I feel that I don't have the option to back down from anything, because ultimately, the outcome is weightless. Nevertheless, I remember growing up with a mild case of asthma and anxiety and I feared death intensely as I constantly struggled to breathe. As a child I always imagined what death was like and how it felt to "disappear" from existence. Up until I experimented with drugs, a dramatic vision of hell haunted me almost nightly up until I became a young adult, then I almost welcomed death comically. I became a heavy drinker to the point where I unconsciously and repetitively would attempt suicide by overdosing daily on drugs and alcohol.

But one morning, I remember having an unforgettable dream in my late teens, one that soothes me to this day. I dreamed that my mother came home and consoled me. It was as unreal as it was the defining moment in my existence, when I no longer feared what is beyond the veil of death but rather embraced poetry to keep track of my emotions. My mother was a deep lover of poetry.

Darius Spearman is a husband, father, educator, and author of *Between the Color Lines: A History of African Americans on the California Frontier From 1769 Through Reconstruction*. He was awarded a Master of Arts degree in history (2000) and education (2006) and joined the faculty of the Department of Black Studies at San Diego City College in 2007.

Darius Spearman
Dueling Consciousness

> *The inability to be vulnerable means that we are unable to feel.
> If we cannot feel we cannot truly emotionally connect with one
> another. We cannot know love.*
>
> —bell hooks, *We Real Cool: Black Men and
> Masculinity,* 2004

Rage. Frustration. Fear. Dejection.

All of these feelings swirled around my brain as I pulled into the parking stall and contemplated my options. It was a familiar place for me. Initially, throwing a tantrum like a two-year-old seemed the only reasonable response to the situation. Even as I felt the urge to destroy everything within arms length, I could simultaneously feel myself reasoning my way out of it.

With you, my son, sitting in the car next to me, flying into a rage was simply not an option. Because of what just happened, I didn't have the luxury of entertaining the possibility of losing (at least the semblance of) my composure.

Stay sharp, Darius! You don't have time for this shit! Instead of smashing the nearest object in my vicinity, I whipped out my phone and began composing an email to your support team: the social worker, therapist, and co-conservator (my wife)—with the subject line: "So, this happened."

I sat in my car composing my email after just having picked you up from a psychiatric program that was supposed to help you with—among other things—impulse control. For that reason, losing my cool was something I could never allow you to see me do. This was the third-string program that I had fought to get you into for treatment for schizoaffective disorder, so I suppose I couldn't blame them. Once again, however, I was being asked to do what so many professionals from whom I had sought help were unable to do—to bring my son back to a manageable state after having suffered a psychotic break. You had become a danger to those around you, but mostly to yourself. I had once again received a frantic call to pick you up from the professionals who were supposed to help you.

I arrived and got the rundown. Apparently, you had threatened to assault the hospital staff, bolted from the program, and you were currently running along the freeway offramp. About four or five of the staff stood around me in a semicircle explaining the situation until they reached the moment in the story where you bolted. At that point, the conversation stopped abruptly. As I leaned forward, my eyes widened as I hung onto their last word. I was expecting at any moment to hear what they were going to do next. Have a staff member follow him at a distance? Alert public safety? Transfer him to a more intensive level psychiatric program? To my horror, it dawned on me that they were finished. They were now waiting for me to tell them what I was going to do. All that was clear was that my son was not to come back to this facility, and they would play no role in where he went from here.

My son was missing, and he was last seen in an agitated state running along the freeway. At five foot seven inches tall, 280 pounds, speech- and language-impaired, and barely able to respond to prompts even when not agitated, this could be an extremely dangerous situation. The thought of someone else, perhaps law enforcement, finding you before I did left me nearly petrified. Focus, Darius! This is no time to fall apart! You don't have time to be afraid!

I returned my attention to the hospital staff, and I channeled the most commanding tone I could muster. "Call 911 right away and let them know that there is someone in the community who probably will not respond to police commands. I don't want my son shot!" With that, I jumped in my car and raced off in the direction that one of the staff members pointed.

As I sped up the hill, I finally had a chance to let my thoughts settle a bit. It must've been less than a minute before I caught up with you, since you were on foot.

That was enough time to remember the day you were born. I saw you as you came out of your mother's womb and was the first to know that you were a boy. I remember telling people that I was no way in hell going to cut the umbilical cord. I was surprised, though, when I found the scissors in my hand snipping away. When you first came out of your mother's womb, you made a face that is difficult to describe. Your face contorted, and your eyes moved wildly one way and your lips pursed wildly the other. You didn't cry. You hardly made a sound.

By age two you were not talking. I was afraid, but the doctors told me not to worry. Even though my feelings told me otherwise, I shoved my fear aside because the doctors told me what I wanted to hear. Finally, when you were still not talking by age three you were diagnosed with autism. Back then autism was just a bullshit term that pediatrics used to indicate a diagnosis of, "We don't know what the fuck is wrong with your kid." Now we have a bit better understanding of what autism is. At the time, however, I wasn't given much information, other than that I was dealing with a developmental disability. Would you be able to lead a productive life? Would you be able to attend school? Be independent? Get married? Would you ever even learn to talk? To each of these, the answer was, "There's no way we can know at this point." I was simply told that you were "in a world of your own." Back then the various programs had wildly different (and often conflicting) approaches to treatment. I was now faced with the fear of the unknown. I was already about a year behind in the diagnosis, though, so I didn't have time for fear. Shoving that fear aside, I made up my mind that I was going to proceed under the assumption that you were going to be okay. If you were going to be okay, I would make it okay.

I was an unstoppable force. Fear would not control me. If anything, fear would be my ally.

Now that autism is better understood, and you have done remarkably well at learning to manage it, we face another challenge that pushes the limitations of current expertise in the field—dual diagnosis. How do we manage and treat autism *and* schizoaffective disorder? All of my attempts to get you into a psychiatric treatment program had been frustrated because those who treat psychiatric disorders do not deal in developmental disabilities and vice versa. The regional center, which I relied upon to manage your autism, would provide no assistance in finding resources for psychiatric disorders. In a Catch-22, I had to settle for the third-string program instead of the more intensive and appropriate programs because they were not equipped to address the needs of patients with autism.

I had worked every angle I could and I simply couldn't get you the services that you needed. Getting you the help that you needed was out of my hands—the same hands that were now fighting the urge to destroy every object in my vicinity. With you sitting next to me, though, after having spent so much time with you to help you develop the skills to manifest your anger in a healthy way, how could I possibly give in to my own anger, fear, and frustration? Besides, I have become so practiced in containing my fear and anger I've all but forgotten how to deal with it emotionally myself. Herein lies my dilemma: now that you were acting out in anger, helping you to express your anger in a healthy way was a task I was not equipped to carry out.

I understand that "acting out" is defined as expressing through actions what you don't have the ability to express in words. With everything you're dealing with now—with no way of understanding why you can't have unlimited amounts of candy, why you don't have a girlfriend, or why your mom threw up her hands and walked away—I've always seen it as my job to help you find the words. I'm not sure why I expected you to get the right answer when I asked you the question this morning, "Do you think it's okay for you to be angry?" My heart sank when you replied, "No."

How could you possibly know that it's okay to be angry and that it's okay to be afraid when that is the one lesson I've never been able to show you by example. Worse yet, how could I teach you how to be afraid when that is something I've never had time to learn myself?

Wilnisha Sutton, also known as TRU7H (Truth), was born in Los Angeles but raised in San Diego. She is now focused on her music career and bettering her future for her son's sake. She's very active in the music scene as well as in her community in Southeast San Diego. She has paid a high price for her past misdemeanor charges. She recently lost a job as a teacher's aide because her background check did not clear within the three-day time frame. It was cleared 30 days later, but that was too late.

Wilnisha "TRU7H" Sutton
This Is the Truth

I dedicate this story to my mother because without her prayers and encouragement I wouldn't be where I am today.

I was in this cell for twenty-two hours out of the day. I had no control over what I could do, when I could eat, or when I could go outside. It fucked me up mentally. I thought to myself, This is slavery. I'm like a rat in a cage. Most of the women in jail were Mexican and black. When a girl would have a little "attitude," or say something sassy, the racist guards would knock her down, grab her, kick her, beat her, you know, "handle without care" and without any respect. The female guards and black guards were the worst. The other girls told me, "Don't mess with these guards." There was a fear of the "massa" and this was in 2006!

I had been in other jails in San Diego where there were junkies everywhere detoxing all around me, where I woke up in the middle of the night, cold and not sure where I was. But I would always see familiar faces, and people who helped raise me at different times of my constantly disrupted childhood. Those places were familiar, but Orange County was a whole other level. In San Diego, at least I wasn't fearful of the guards. In Orange County, I was terrified.

I'd only been to jail a few times but all my charges were related to the same thing, prostitution. I always did three or four days because I always seemed to go to jail on a holiday weekend. But these fourteen days were killer. Might not seem like much to some, but to me it was enough. Since my case wasn't violent, on my seventh day they moved me to a camp. I met other girls who were also from San Diego and who were also in the game. So we talked about our pimps, and told each other stories. They told me the rules of the camp, and I was just happy we got to go outside. I was happy to smell the trees, feel the air blow on my neck, and just be under the sun. I'd taken these things for granted when I was free, and I never took the time to just relax and notice, 'cause I was always chasing money but never seemed to catch enough.

At the age of 18, I did *not* know how to sit my ass down. My childhood had been chaos. I lived with different family members, I moved constantly, I changed schools often and I made friends, but lost contact. I didn't feel loved and I didn't feel safe because I wasn't with my mom. I was born in the '80s when most of our parents were addicted to crack cocaine. My mom was around but she wasn't capable of being there for me because of her drug addiction. She signed over her parental rights while she was in jail. I was never comfortable as a kid, and by the time my mom got her stuff together, I had already created my patterns of staying on the go so I never had to really deal with my pain. I didn't slow down, and I didn't reflect on what I had been through. I just kept adding more bullshit to my chaos and I began to perpetuate my family's cycle of addiction. Ecstasy, feeling loved, and music were my addictions.

I thought Matthew was the love of my life. He had a charismatic vibe that was attractive to me. In fact, he was attractive to a lot of other females too. He was good with words, he dressed nice, he sang well, smelled delicious; we had great sex and he knew a lot about the game. He knew I was a lost, vulnerable girl on ecstasy. I told him my whole life story the first night and he listened. He listened well. I was willing to do whatever it took to be around him.

I had previous experience with a pimp, but now I chose to pay Matthew. I paid him *everything* I made. I never disrespected him by talking to other pimps. I always represented him as being the pimp he wanted to be portrayed as. I held on to every word he said. Once, he told me to stand on the corner, and I did. He even beat me up one time at the trolley station because another pimp said I "was out o' pocket." But behind closed doors, he was a sweet guy. He was conflicted and lost and I saw the potential of what he could have been in spite of the beatings and sexual violence. Ecstasy and the music we were listening to made everything seem right. We listened to rap music that was centered on pimpin', so my life with Matthew and his abuse seemed like the norm.

Part of the game was to always stay on the go, wherever the money was at. One night we would be in San Diego, the next in Las Vegas, or Miami. Also, havin' multiple hoes meant more money, so Matthew was always searchin' for different bitches and we were always traveling around. I'll never forget the night before I went to jail in Orange County because that was when Matthew and I got into a huge fight.

Normally I'm able to control my emotions enough to not talk or fight back, but this time, and every time after, I fought. This time, I lost it. It was the fact that he had found a new bitch—shapely, and light-skinned with curly long hair—and him staying in the room with this bitch we had just met while I was out getting his money made me crazy. I mean I still made money, but I couldn't think straight wondering what they were doing. He neglected his pimp responsibilities. I had been followed and almost sexually assaulted a few nights before by a random guy, yet Matthew wasn't out watching me 'cause he was in the hotel room with her. When I returned to the room, my attitude was horrible for the rest of the night. She didn't notice, but he did. Matthew went to sleep while she told me her whole life story that night. She wasn't trying to get with the program and make some money. She just wanted to have fun. I was very territorial so I wasn't going to make it easy for her to be around him for free when I had to pay. She woke up early and left. He woke me up screaming that I ran her off. I acted like I didn't hear him, but once he started pouring a gallon of water on the top of my head, I lost it. I punched, kicked, screamed, broke lamps, tables and chairs. I threw every hygiene product I could find at him and he cried like a baby. He wasn't used to me acting this way. I went from total submission to finding some strength. He called my mom and begged her to come and get me. She did.

I wasn't on my toes the next night. My shoes weren't laced as tight as they should have been. I was definitely caught slipping. My emotions were everywhere because I had just got into a huge fight with the guy I thought was the "love of my life" and I just wasn't myself. Matthew called me the whole time I was there, telling me to just come home, but I was tired of going back and forth with him. I went to Orange County and I just wanted to get some money. The crazy thing about the hoe stroll there was that it was on the same exact street as Disneyland. Daddy came to play while Mommy and the kids slept. All he had to do was drive a mile down to find many flavors, ages and shapes of females to pick to play with. All he needed was money and he could be the Mickey in his own Disneyland.

But I was so out of it that I got caught up in a sting, and that's how I ended up in jail.

The prostitutes ended up in jail, and the Johns stayed a few hours and went back to their wives.

El Cajon Boulevard, San Diego

I knew something drastic was coming because I had a dream I couldn't shake a few days before going to jail. This dream wasn't like any other dream. I felt it in the pit of my stomach. In the dream, my mother had died in a car accident and so I woke up crying. I prayed right before I went out to El Cajon Blvd, which was one of the hoe strolls in my city. I never lost my faith even though I lost my way. When I got to the blade (which is another word for hoe stroll) I set up shop in front of this bus stop that was close to the corner. I'd leave and walk around but I was getting lucky sitting there. So I figured I might as well work it until I couldn't. Cars kept coming and pulling into the Blockbuster that was right behind the bus stop. I made the most money I had ever made on that boulevard that night. Matthew wasn't around. He was on the streets somewhere but I couldn't find him. We had Boost Mobile walkie-talkie phones that had just run out of minutes. So after my first date, I was going to put minutes on both of our phones, but when I went to 7-11 the Boost Mobile system was down. I'd have each date drop me off at the 7-11, but it stayed down all morning. Around 4 a.m. I was in a daze, worried about where Matthew was, as I sat at the bus stop. We had no way to communicate and he was my lifeline. I stayed down (out there) for at least seven or eight hours. Then something told me to get up and walk to the corner, which, still in a daze, I did. I snapped out of it once I heard the sound of a Cadillac and Dodge van crashing into each other. The Cadillac spun into the bus stop and completely destroyed it. The van spun right in front of me and I had to jump back so I wouldn't get hit. So much glass was in my legs and I just walked away crying. I paid no mind to the pimp yelling out his window, "If you were my hoe I wouldn't have you crying." I just needed to get away from the car crash. I walked two blocks and ran into Matthew. He asked me why I was crying and I told him. I handed him all the money I made and then we left.

In retrospect I interpret that dream as the old me dying and the new me about to be born. It was a sign that I'd soon become a mother. My pregnancy forced me to finally slow down and focus. I decided to quit the game and started going to San Diego City College to pursue my dream, which was singing. I got a job canvassing for political propositions and that helped the activist in me awaken. Now I'm involved heavily in my community and will continue to fight the good fight.

I'm still in the process of rewiring my brain and recovering from the fog of my addiction to the attractions of "the game," the music, the ecstasy, and desire to be loved.

But This Is the Truth

I believed I was making a choice. I believed it was okay for him to beat me and mentally abuse me. I believed it was right to give him all the money I made on the streets. I believed that it was about love. I was wrong. He was criminal. He was misogynistic. He exploited me, and he was sick. The type of rap music I was addicted to brainwashed me as it has brainwashed so many of us—both brothers *and* sisters.

I must continue to stay in my lane and move forward. I know what my purpose is and I won't allow anything to stop me. I now reach out to girls who are still lost in the "lifestyle," the euphemism for a life of enduring physical and mental abuse, exploitation, emotional manipulation, and loss of self-worth.

Samantha Jasmine was born in Detroit, Michigan. She moved to San Diego, California for ministry purposes in September of 2001. Currently Samantha is a student at San Diego City College, finishing up her associate degree in allied health and biology, and plans to transfer to Fisk University to finish her bachelor's degree in nursing. Samantha is a former president of the San Diego City College chapter of Umoja and is a peer mentor for new Umoja students. She is very involved with the Associated Student Government on campus, is an active member of Grace Covenant Christian Church, and is a member of Pillars of the Community. She is very involved with her academic, spiritual and local community.

Samantha Jasmine

Welcome to Blessed Like Dat's Winter Wonderland

A Peek in My Alabaster Box

I would like to dedicate this story to my Sweet Pea, my angel and inspiration for what I do. I would also like to dedicate this story to Professor Detroit for believing in me and helping ensure that my story got out—I love you, Mona. And lastly, to Professor Alexander—thanks OG for helping reintroduce me to Samantha, the writer.

"Dr. Schiff, do you think it's possible for Sweet Pea to travel to Detroit this year for Christmas? He has never seen snow, and I would like to take him home for Christmas. It's on his bucket list and if it's really true what you say about his illness, I would like to grant that wish for him."

The doctors had told me that my son didn't have long to live—but I didn't accept that truth because I needed to stay hopeful. Cancer, acute lymphoblastic leukemia to be exact, would ultimately claim his life. "Mrs. Thornton, as much as I would love to say yes, he is not even well enough to leave the hospital, let alone travel to Detroit. I'm sorry, but this trip won't be possible." I walked out of the room feeling so bummed. What was I going to tell Sweet Pea? I couldn't break his heart; he was so looking forward to this trip!

I walked into my son's room and looked into those big, beautiful, brown eyes. He excitedly asked, "Soooooooo, Sugga Momma, what did Dr. Shanekwa say?" That's what he called his doctor; he named her after his favorite cartoon character from the Backyardigans. "When do we leave?" "Well, Sweet Pea, we can leave as soon as we close our eyes!" With the most puzzled look on his face, he asked, "Huh? What's that suppose to mean?" "It means that we will use our IMAGINATION!"

Over the next 24 hours, I began to brainstorm how I was going to make this vision such a reality that it really felt like Christmas in Detroit, but without having to buy that expensive plane ticket or deal with The Hawk for real. If you ever been to Detroit in the winter, you know what I am talking about. First, I went to Walmart and paced up and down the aisle as I tried to figure out how to make the scene feel real. I was pretty bummed myself, but there was no way I could let Sweet Pea feel my frustration. "Hmmmmm, how can I make him understand the concept of snow?" *Brain SURGE!* I got some cotton and a squirt bottle. I started loading bags and bags of cotton in my cart, at least 15.

Ideas started pouring in my head! I got different types of ornaments for icicles, air freshener that smelled like pine and frankincense, some fake pine trees because real plants and trees were not allowed at his hospital ward due to the children's immune systems being compromised because of cancer and blood disorders. I got large, life-size candy canes for the life-size sled that we would build in his room. I bought light-up reindeer and light-up penguins because my son loved penguins. I grabbed a huge Christmas bell to hang on the front of his door and a nice, big, red cover for his bed, which would be converted into a sleigh. I found some garland, candy canes and I bought stuff to make a gingerbread house. Last but not least, I bought him a coat, winter gloves, and a Spider-Man hat and scarf set. To make the scene more realistic, I grabbed white spray paint for the frost effect for the windows. As I walked to the checkout lane, I whispered under my breath, "God, I need this stuff to come to life; I need my Sweet Pea to feel like he is really in a winter wonderland."

As I drove back to the hospital, I started getting very excited. I may not be able to fly my baby home, but I am gonna make sure he feels like he's home. Back at the hospital, I grabbed a wagon and filled it with everything

I had just bought and rushed to Sweet Pea's room. I cracked the door and saw him sitting up in his bed with the biggest grin on his face. This was a big deal because at this point, he couldn't walk or do much for himself. He said, "Sugga Momma, what's all that cool stuff you got?" I happily replied, "It's all for you, so your room can come alive!" He replied sarcastically, "I didn't know it was dead." I laughed and said, "Touché!"

My sis, Reda, and I began decorating his room. We hung ornaments from the ceiling to give the illusion of icicles. I busted open ten huge bags of cotton and spread the cotton balls all over the room and gave the rest of the cotton to Sweet Pea. Of course he asked, "What's this for?" I said, "So you can make snowballs and a snowman!" Puzzled, he asked, "Snowball, what's that?" I said, "They are balls made of snow. Let me show you how to make one." I rolled the cotton into a ball and once I had a good enough size I sprayed it with water and threw it at him. The look on his face was priceless. "Sugga Momma! Why did you do that? It's wet!" I said, "We are having a snowball fight later and I just wanted you to know what to look forward to." "Hmmmmm, I don't know if I like it yet," he said. I said, "Trust me, you will."

For about three more hours, Reda and I worked on his room, and by the time we were done, we had a live sleigh, snow, snowmen, trees, penguins and reindeer all over the room. There were icicles hanging from the ceiling, and to top it off, I turned the air down to arctic levels. I sprayed the room with pine and I kept a burner with frankincense burning so it smelled like Christmas, or at least what I thought Christmas should smell like. Sweet Pea had fallen asleep while we were working and I was glad because he was going to wake up in a different city than the one he went to sleep in.

Finally, 3:15 a.m. rolled around and it was time for his meds. Nurse Cindy, his favorite nurse, walked in and stood in awe of our work. She looked around, and the expression on her face said: Wow, Mom, you did a great job! With wide eyes, she exclaimed, "What did I just step into?"

I said, "Blessed Like Dat's Winter Wonderland, aka Detroit." Then she said, "Why is it so cold in here? We need some heat."

I smiled. I had more than accomplished my goal. I had convinced an adult who definitely knew we were in San Diego that she had been transported to Detroit in a matter of hours. She even noticed that I had put a pair of reindeer ears on Sweet Pea. She said, "How adorable! He is the cutest reindeer I have ever seen! How did you come up with this? Can you come decorate my house? I need to go get my phone so I can take a picture. This is awesome!"

This act of love for my son spread like wildfire. Other parents began to approach me for help; they wanted to turn their child's room into something other than a place of sickness and disease. My favorite was Baby Carly. She was the cutest little girl, with big, blue eyes that could light up any room, the fattest little cheeks, golden blonde hair, and a precious little voice. She was diagnosed with neurosarcoma, a malignant growth composed of neural, connective and vascular tissues, mostly known as a malignant sheath tumor. Oh, and did I mention that she was just thirteen months old? Her situation broke my heart because she was even younger than my son when he was diagnosed. She was barely a year old. Just like me, Baby Carly's Mom was a single parent because her husband was incarcerated. So naturally, her mom and I quickly connected.

Of course, because I like being unique, I told her that she could not have the same winter wonderland that was exclusive for my Sweet Pea; however, I assured her we could brainstorm ideas how to make Baby Carly's room come to life as well. After sitting and talking for a while, we came up with a theme for her room: "The gift of healing" because her daughter was freshly diagnosed, and it can be quite devastating to hear that kind of heavy news about your child, especially around the holidays. Carly loved the color blue, so her theme colors were royal blue and icicle silver. I began by wrapping all types of boxes. I hung several of them from the ceiling and left some of the boxes open and placed them all around the room. Inside the open boxes we placed cards with healing prayers that we wrote, the names of her doctors, chemo support family and friends. These were what I considered her gifts of healing.

I can't even begin to tell you how wonderful I felt to be able to give back like that in such a trying time in both of our lives. Not only did I help my son experience one of his lifetime wishes, but I also helped another parent in need. I would have never been able to do that from Detroit. They say that you will know we are Christians by our love. Well, this was definitely an act of love. I was experiencing my own personal storm and I reached out to someone else in need instead of focusing on my own problems. Because of how I have been blessed and seen God move in my life, and the way my personality is, there was no way I could not help. I knew that giving my time and talents sometimes means more than money. In this case, money would not have helped anyway.

I wanted to honor Sweet Pea's wishes. He was my only child, and if in fact I didn't have long with him, I wanted him to have the best quality of life possible. I have beautiful memories of this winter wonderland not only because of his room but because it was my last Christmas with him. A lot of people just gave up and accepted what these doctors told them about their loved ones, but not me. I never back down from a challenge. I am a thermostat not a thermometer, which means a thermometer takes the temperature while a thermostat regulates the temperature. I give life to a situation rather than have it taken from me. Cancer was just something we had to deal with in our lives, but it was not my life. As my granny used to always tell me: "When life throws you lemons, make lemonade; and I like mine sweet, so throw some strawberries in there." She would also remind me that when life seems like it's trying to break you, tie a knot in the rope and reach beyond the break and keep going. Being told I couldn't take him home was my break in the rope. His winter wonderland was tying my knot and reaching beyond it to keep moving. I hope that by letting you take a peek in my alabaster box, you see that with God nothing is impossible, but with him all things are possible. Amen.

Photo: Sarah Loud

Zenia E. Torres was born in Riverside but raised in San Diego. She is currently fulfilling her role as a mother to a beautiful, bright young boy while working on finishing her AA degree in psychology at San Diego City College. Her dream is to transfer to San Diego State University, but her ultimate goal in life is to help others and to give back to her communities. Stay tuned....

Zenia Torres
For the Love of Math

I would like to dedicate this story to my son. I want him to know that no matter what obstacles we may face we can and will overcome.

It was already bad enough that I was going to a school I didn't quite fit into. Beige tones were the predominant flesh color walking around. Brand labels on full display and $$$ signs were very apparent. I didn't want to attend an "inner city" school. That was a term I didn't learn until I was actually in my third year of high school only because someone told me that I was a product of a low-funded, underrepresented environment.

After we had been taken away from my mother because of her substance abuse problem and cases of domestic violence, we had finished our year detour with a few months' stay at the Polinski Center and a half-year stay with two sets of foster parents. Our first foster parent was evil, but the second one—God bless Gloria, she was an angel.

My father had used that year to get his shit together. Finally, we were going home. I mean not really, but at least it was with my father. We were moving to City Heights off of Highland Ave. into my father's one-bedroom apartment. When my brother and I arrived, we weren't expecting what we found. We weren't used to those new living conditions. All kinds of people hung around that place; there were drugs, prostitutes, and crime. And then there was Angela, with her two small kids who had eggs on their little heads that belonged to the invading lice crawling all over their scalps. I feel itchy just thinking about it, and I remember thinking to myself that I had to avoid them at all costs! There was no

good place to play in the complex, unless I was three houses down playing with Vanessa. Her grandma was the best. It was a nice escape.

Living with my mother, we never had much money, but we lived
across the street from Golden Hill Park. We saw trees every day and had
friendly neighbors. Even before the gentrification, with Lomas gang-
bangers marking the street walls, it was still better than this. Both my
brother and I had performed in the Fern Street Circus and I had been
involved in ballet, tap, and jazz. Golden Hill was home. What was this?

I had finished middle school kind of half-assedly. I realized living with
my dad was only 20 percent better than living with my mom, because he
too is an alcoholic. That kind of ruined the "better life" idea I had pic-
tured for my brother and me. I don't even remember why I had filled out
the school choice form. At just 13 years old I had taken the initiative to
fill out this form so that I could have the opportunity to go to any high
school outside of the "inner city." I needed an escape from the reality
that was beginning to unfold. I didn't want to be like my parents and I
still don't want to be. I wanted to be something more. Having the option
to leave that neighborhood, even if it was just for eight hours a day, was
going to be my ticket out, an exit. I didn't take into consideration how
attending an affluent school would affect me or my learning process. I
didn't fit in: my clothing was off, and my hair was wild and coarse. My
accent was in full cholita mode, and my poorness exuded from the pores
of my brown skin. I had been taking care of my brother since the age of
seven and still am. I had grown up on my own and I did not take kindly
to people telling me what to do. What could they tell me about me?
Absolutely nothing!

His name was Dr. King and we had to call him that or Professor.
Dr. King was a six-foot white man with short spiky blonde hair buzzed
off on the sides. His staple outfit was always the same: shorts that hit
mid-calf and a short-sleeve polo with three little buttons going down
the middle. And how to forget the old white "dad sneakers" he used to

sport with white socks that met those shorts. He was a self-proclaimed "All-American War Hero" throwing his white privilege in my face. He had served his country in the most honorable way possible, and because of that, we had to hold him on the highest of pedestals. He spoke about his career and how much good he had done for the world but I wasn't really buying any of it. If anything, I thought it was more arrogant than heroic. I didn't understand why he was showing off to us. I began to tune him out because none of it was a benefit to me or my life. What did his "legacy" have to do with me?

One day I began to tune out the "professor's" spiel and let my mind wander. I realized a few minutes later that he had stopped speaking, and when I looked up, I saw his round belly hanging over my desk. We made eye contact and all I could remember feeling is that I had unintentionally "disrespected" him by not hanging on his every word. I don't even remember the words that were exchanged but it was the beginning of my subconscious hatred for math.

All I care to remember from that point was how I was viewed and dealt with on a daily basis. I had defied Dr. King's authority and he had despised every minute of it. Chewing gum—referral, go to the office; speaking too loudly—referral, go to the office; forgetting to raise my hand—referral, go to the office; rolling my eyes—referral, go to the office. After a while it just became routine. The office had become my classroom and eventually I was given packets of math work to complete by the end of the week. There was no one to talk to, no one to ask questions, no one to ask me if I needed help or if I understood the material. I mean, it's not that I couldn't do the work; I had tested into GATE, for crying out loud. The work was easy, but I was no longer interested. How could I be when I had been so easily removed from my classroom without a single thought as to why I was displaying that behavior in the first place? If they didn't care about me, why should I care about learning math? Dr. King's disposing of "the problematic child," basically throwing me away, was probably the biggest reason why there has been a huge disconnect between math and me.

I didn't realize the effect of this experience until I had become a 26-year-old adult. I'm a bit wiser now and I don't know what I'm going to do with this information, but maybe this insight can lead me to grow from it. I don't want to hate math anymore, because I want to understand it.

Fast forward to 2016.... I'm just about to reach my goal as graduation is on the horizon. I can see it now. All that stands between me and my goal is math. How ironic that something from so long ago still hinders my chances of success. I guess it's a good thing that resiliency came out of all of this. I imagine myself walking across that stage in my cap and gown, and that vision alone will be the reason I make it.

Alberto Vasquez is currently a graduate candidate at University of California, San Diego, pursuing a master's degree in biology. Beto is a first-generation college student and a father of four. He is committed to becoming a community college professor of biology and ultimately an administrator of higher education. He has worked as a substance abuse counselor and has years of experience working with at-risk populations. Having experienced a life of incarceration himself (juvenile, county and state), he is all too familiar with the multifaceted challenges faced by this demographic.

Alberto "Beto" Vasquez
You Work Here?

Special thanks to my family—that of blood and of spirit.

Mistakes do not define who you are,
and your past does not dictate your future.

I remember participating in my first laboratory research internship and can easily relive the first day my eyes opened up to this experience which I would have never imagined possible.

It was summer 2011; I was accepted into the Center for Systems biology program at UCSD. Up to then, I had merely fulfilled a role as an actor, portraying the role of a student. After all, there were only three reasons why I had decided to attend college: collect financial aid, meet people and stay out of trouble. I was informed by Cookie, the program coordinator, that after much deliberation I had been selected in the Center's summer program. She would later inform me that she had fought hard for my selection because my story reminded her of her brother, a story redolent with challenges and desperation. I was overwhelmed by her honesty and support—which I rarely received from my own family growing up.

As the start date drew near, I was informed that I would have to select a lab to work in and was provided a list of potential host labs to choose from. These labs varied in specialty and areas of interest, most of which I wasn't the least bit familiar with. For the past 15 years my acquaintance with lab equipment included the heating and cooling process of Pyrex to make paraphernalia to indulge in my extra-curricular activities. Now I had to choose what kind of research work I wanted to do in areas like genomics, proteomics, spatiotemporal architecture, cell-to-cell communication and other difficult things to pronounce. I was elated, yet fearful of what was to come. So after much deliberation and seeking the infinite wisdom of Google, I was left to employ the only course of action that made sense. I looked at the pictures of the labs I was offered and went with the lab where I saw the staff smiling, the lab of Elizabeth Winzeler, Ph.D. My only encounters with *plasmodium*, or malaria, had been on television. After all, in this country we only really concern ourselves with first-world problems like wifi speed or online presence. Now I was researching this cunning disease that plagues so many underdeveloped countries and claims hundreds of thousands of lives, many of them children. How could it be that this vato, who was the first in his family to attempt this college thing, could be provided such an opportunity? Surely they had made a mistake—or had they?

I was raised in a neighborhood with scarred sidewalks, marked by hopeless vision and complacency. I still ask myself how I ended up here. I didn't know anyone who went to college, let alone someone who worked in a laboratory. Before this, my only experience of being in a lab was when I had to visit the phlebotomist to give some blood and satiate a doctor's request. Then again, these were also few and far between, given that I didn't have health coverage growing up.

Now, here I am. In my early thirties, on North Torrey Pines Road, in La Jolla, where even the air smells different, in a facility belonging to the world-renowned Scripps Research Institute. I would conduct biomolecular research on pathogens and the development of antimalarial drugs.

I had many reservations about the venture I was about to embark upon. I couldn't figure out why I was so nervous about this and how I had been much less worried about more volatile, life-threatening situations in the past. After years of chemical abuse, prison riots, shootings, risky behaviors and near-death accidents, I should have been dead. Was I scared to fail, or was fear grounded in success?

Unsure, but willing to expose myself to new things in life, I proceeded. After all, if I expected new outcomes I had to try new things.

Regardless of what I looked like, where I had grown up or my academic standing, I was well received in this new environment. I was quickly shown around and familiarized with all the gadgets and lab equipment, things that turned, gyrated, whirled, adjusted temperatures and ultimately contributed to scientific inquiry. Here laid undiscovered scientific findings that would someday alter life—or help save it. I was now part of this scientific process. Any pressure I felt was my very own, because I didn't know how I was supposed to respond to this newfound opportunity. What was I expected to know? What was I, this Chicano kid from Barrio Logan, supposed to contribute? Interestingly, these same questions continue to haunt me. I am no stranger to feelings of inadequacy and doubt. What is different is that I have learned how to drown out adversities with hope, which, in the end, is much louder. I had to have something to offer, right? Otherwise why would I have made it this far? How could I have made it into a graduate program in biology at one of the most academically rigorous research-based institutions in the world if I didn't have what it takes? On some level, these thoughts were the same I experienced when I was last paroled from prison; would I make it this time? I sure hoped so.

The weeks flew by and I quickly adjusted. Being a tactile learner I quickly got the hang of things and familiarized myself with routine tasks and experimental techniques. In no time I was on my way to developing my summer research project, discovering my findings and organizing my thoughts for my upcoming presentation. It was not out of the ordinary to spend countless hours in the lab. As a matter of fact, I was often the first one in the lab, especially during the time I was assigned to cover one of the scientist's tasks while she was away. As I was responsible for para-sitting (that is, parasite-babysitting), I would show up early in the morning or on the weekends to feed, change and nurture our growing strains of inoculated parasites that would later be used to further compound studies. Some mornings I would be the only one in the lab, accompanied only by maintenance staff. In those few short weeks I couldn't help but notice that the only Latino folks here were either custodial or facilities staff. Everyone I worked with in this lab was either European, Asian or white. Although I never really tripped on this, subconsciously I was very aware, and this would heighten my desire to excel.

One morning, while preparing for an assay in my bench area, I was caught off guard by an interesting encounter. I had just prepared my cup of coffee and was headed to my work area when a Mexican man approached me. This man would regularly come in to fill up the various gas tanks that we used in the labs (nitrogen, oxygen, etc.). As was common practice, and continues to be, being the minority in situations, I organically tend to attempt to connect with others who look like me, culturally or sub-culturally. In a subtle attempt to connect I proceeded with the usual courtesy, by nodding my head in acknowledgement as if to say, "I see you and you are deserving of the same hospitality I would extend anyone here." After all, growing up I had been taught to treat all people as human, sharing the same dignity and respect for the transients in the alleys as well as any professional person. Incarceration had further instilled in me the importance of acknowledging folks regardless of their position. On this momentous occasion I was stopped in my tracks when this man whom I had never conversed with beyond pleasantries stopped, turned to me and asked, "Do you work here?" Stunned and unclear about his question, I responded, "Yes, why?"

Intrigued, he continued to ask, "But you don't just clean here, you actually work here?"

I reassured him once again that I worked as a research assistant.

His response would leave a resonating impression upon me for the rest of my life. Elated, this stranger quickly shouted out to his work partner, who was a white man, and said, "See, I told you we have representation in here and not just cleaning!"

Seeing the surprise on my face, he explained that his white counterpart had expressed that he had never seen any Mexicans (specifically) working in the labs they serviced. Well, he wouldn't be able to say that anymore.

I was excited and stunned by this entire experience. Why were we seen in supporting roles but not leading ones? Why is it that we, people of color, don't strive to excel in STEM-related fields?

Maybe it's for the same reason that the importance of reading was never emphasized in my home. Maybe it's because my parents grew up in extreme poverty where the need to survive overwhelmed the desire to dream for more. Maybe my family was ignorant or just lacked the social capital to strive for more. Who knows?

One thing is certain: my children will not experience that. They will be exposed to labs, science and higher education early on and will have access to tap into my social capital. It is my civic obligation to share my experience and struggles to cultivate tomorrow's leaders and the next generation of scientists, engineers and mathematicians, both in my home and in my community.

additional resources

Darius Spearman

Reclaiming Our Stories: A Historical Overview

The stories compiled in this volume are set against a backdrop woven out of an era of political conservatism. By the late 1970s, the backlash against the gains of the civil rights movement and President Johnson's "war on poverty" were well underway. In 1978, the Supreme Court heard the case of *Regents of the University of California v. Bakke*,[1] which launched the assault against affirmative action and ushered in an era of "personal responsibility" and "colorblindness." Throughout the 1980s, Ronald Reagan gave the notion of a "colorblind" society mass appeal to the broader American public through his ability to shift the focus of public discourse.[2] Having hijacked the stories of the poor and communities of color for political gain, Democratic and Republican administrations alike peddled a story that characterized the poor as simply lazy and singularly focused on gaming the system. Coded terms such as "welfare queen," "crack mother," and "superpredator" racialized poverty and turned the tide of public sentiment against public assistance for the poor and toward more punitive approaches that all but criminalized poverty. Politicians from Reagan through the current Obama administration

---

1   In *Regents of the University of California v. Bakke* (1978), the Supreme Court ruled 5-4 against the use of quotas in the University of California admission system. Leaving open the possibility of other non-quota-based affirmative action programs, however, the court also ruled that the state "has a legitimate and substantial interest in...eliminating...the disabling effects of identified discrimination." There were six different opinions issued by the court including a strongly worded dissent by Justice Thurgood Marshall.

2   Please see "The Conservative Era From Reagan to Obama" in *African Elements*. Online lecture available at http://africanelements.org/episode-14/.

have since cashed in on the political capital of being "tough on crime," giving rise to and perpetuating the prison industrial complex. Between 1980 and 2000, the nation's prison and jail population ballooned from roughly 300,000 to more than 2 million—a staggering 567% increase[3]— but the impacts go far beyond simply incarcerating masses of people.

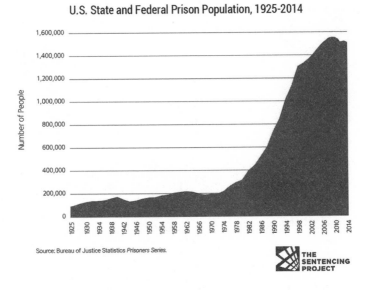

U.S. State and Federal Prison Population, 1925-2014

Source: Bureau of Justice Statistics *Prisoners Series*.

THE SENTENCING PROJECT

The neoconservative agenda continued under Presidents George Bush Sr. and Bill Clinton. Clinton, riding the wave of public backlash against the poor and people of color, promised to "end welfare as we know it." He did so with passage of the Personal Responsibility and Work Opportunity Reconciliation Act of 1996—notice here, the emphasis on personal responsibility. In other words, rather than framing poverty as an economic state of being, poverty was pathologized as a character defect. The most significant piece of legislation passed during the 104th Congress abandoned a guarantee of assistance to poor families. Instead, a

---

3 Michelle Alexander, *The New Jim Crow: Mass Incarceration in the Age of Colorblindness*, p. 59.

wave of punitive measures was put in place that in effect punished the poor simply for being poor.[4]

John J. Dilulio, of the conservative think tank The Manhattan Institute, coined the term "superpredator" in the early 1990s. With this label, many poor and urban youth of color were hyper-criminalized, and thus harsh and punitive policies had to be created to "'deter' and 'incapacitate' them at as an early age as possible."[5] The label superpredator "[t]hrives on the notion that African American and Latino youth are hopeless—thus there is no reason to invest in long-term strategies for youth habilitation and development."[6] As such, the superpredator trope paved the way for the prison industrial complex as a response to the social problems created in the wake of the shift in social policy away from the social justice agenda of the civil rights era to the "personal responsibility" era of the neoconservative movement.

Natalie J. Sokoloff describes the prison industrial complex as a set of bureaucratic, economic, and political interests that encourage spending on prisons, regardless of need.[7] It is rooted in what many scholars have come to understand as "governance through crime," or "the everyday effect that citizens experience from encounters with a society obsessed with surveillance, security, and punitive penal practices."[8] Victor Rios notes that the focus on hyper-punitive policies "stems not from an increase in crime but from the failure of traditional institutions of governance like the welfare state, labor market, and education system...."[9] Thus, mass incarceration entails more than simply incarcerating the masses. It means to subject poor communities and communities of color

4   Barbara Ehrenreich, *The Atlantic*, "It Is Expensive to Be Poor," January 13, 2014. Accessed May 22, 2016 from http://www.theatlantic.com/business/archive/2014/01/it-is-expensive-to-be-poor/282979/.
5   Manny Marable, *Racializing Justice, Disenfranchising Lives: The Racism, Criminal Justice, and Law Reader*, p. 29.
6   Marable, p. 327.
7   Marable, pp. 73-74.
8   Marable, p. 21.
9   Marable, p. 21.

to a complex web of corporate and political interests that redefines them, siphons off both human and monetary capital from them, and exacerbates additional problems of crime, abuse, and addiction.

Using the political machinery of the prison industrial complex the narrative of black, brown, indigenous, and immigrant peoples has been reframed through the lens of white supremacy. In that respect, immigrant communities, communities of color, and even the indigenous communities of the Hawaiian Islands experience a quasi-colonial relationship with the institutions that govern them. It is colonial in the sense that the rules that govern their lives are forged outside of their communities and based on the definitions that are imposed on them, rules that can strip them of their right to due process. Routinely, for example, immigrant detainees and people perceived to be "foreign" are readily stripped of due process simply by virtue of their being labeled immigrants, whether undocumented or not. In San Diego, for example, the family of Anastasio Hernandez Rojas is still seeking justice for the 42-year-old father of five who was tasered and beaten to death by border patrol agents at the US–Mexico border.[10]

Through other means, communities of color—particularly in the area of Southeast San Diego—are subject to a separate set of rules by virtue of their communities being defined by the outside establishment areas of "gang activity." By virtue of nine criteria established solely by the San Diego Police Department's Street Gang Unit, an individual can be proclaimed a gang member if "he or she has three separate contacts with police meeting one or more of the criteria listed" or "one contact with three or more of criteria listed."[11] Persons meeting the deliberately broad criteria are likely to find themselves subject to arbitrary detention, arrest,

---

10 *Democracy Now!* "Cornel West and Carl Dix on Race and Politics in the Age of Obama," July 22, 2009. Retrieved May 22, 2016 from http://www.democracynow.org/2009/7/22/cornel_west_and_carl_dix_on.
11 City of San Diego, "Frequently Asked Questions Regarding Identifying Gangs and Gang Members."

and harsh sentencing enhancements. Just two examples of these criteria are, "Subject has been seen frequenting gang areas," and, "Subject has been seen wearing gang dress."

Although the over-policing and incarceration of communities of color is ostensibly a measure to curtail crime in these communities, research suggests that the far-reaching impacts may in fact exacerbate crime rates. As a result of stress created on families impacted by mass incarceration and the siphoning off of human and monetary resources from the community, "there is a 'tipping point,' after which the number of people in prison is too high so that crime is furthered rather than prevented by incarceration."[12] While it may seem counterintuitive, the "tipping point" is a result of the shift in population from the largely urban to largely rural regions in which the prisons are located.

> The U.S. Bureau of the Census redefines prisoners from poor urban minority communities as living in the region in which they are imprisoned (which is usually far from their homes). The law then transfers funds from the prisoner's home community to the community in which the prison resides, thereby taking much-needed funds from home communities while the prisoner is locked away and unable to contribute to his or her family.[13]

Thus, the census data (and apportionment funds associated with it) is skewed away from the communities subject to incarceration, siphoning off much-needed funding for education, mental health services, and other vital community resources and the very communities in which they are most needed.

The need for increased services was readily apparent in November 2008 when the city of San Diego threatened the closure of nine libraries. Upon hearing of the planned closure, the community of Logan Heights

12 Marable, p. 81.
13 Marable, p. 80.

came together in a massive demonstration and letter-writing campaign to save what it considered to be a valuable community resource—the Beckwourth Library.[14] The community did so recognizing that:

> [I]n addition to providing public access to the internet in places such as libraries, schools, and community technology centers, public policy should invest in training and education services to equip inexperienced internet and computer users with the means to take full advantage of what these technologies have to offer.[15]

As a form of community capital, Beckwourth Library provides the physical space for life skills training (youth development workshops, and counseling), community partnerships (community resources that provide training ground and support), and mentoring (one-on-one relationships between youth and positive adults who can provide guidance, friendship, and positive role-modeling). Over 80% of the youth involved in mentoring stay out of trouble, do better in school, and have a better outlook on life.[16]

Many assumed that the election of Barack Obama would bring the conservative era to a close. As many have pointed out, much of Obama's rhetoric has carried the torch of neo-conservatism. When speaking to black audiences, he has often pathologized the youth by admonishing them to "pull up their pants" while admonishing the parents for not reading to their children or for having children out of wedlock.[17] While many acknowledge Obama's points and few would argue that reading to one's children is necessarily a negative thing, many have also found his

---

14 Darius Spearman, *African Elements*, "An Open Letter to the Leadership of the City of San Diego Originally Published on November 24, 2008," May 27, 2016. Retrieved May 27, 2016 from http://africanelements.org/below-is-an-open-letter-to-the-leadership-of-the-city-of-san-diego-originally-published-on-november-24-2008/.
15 Tavis Smiley, *Covenant With Black America*, p. 228. NOTE: There is an updated version of this text available.
16 Marable, p. 332.
17 *Democracy Now!*

comments particularly callous given the rampant closure of libraries and resources in black and brown communities.

Being read to as children would not have saved the lives of Mike Brown and Treyvon Martin. It is faulty to think that, if only these "thugs" had not worn a hoodie, had not worn sagging pants, had not been walking around at night, etcetera, they would not have been killed. To counter this narrative of who we are, rather than waiting for a representative of political power to challenge the neoconservative narrative, *Reclaiming Our Stories* seeks to take back our identities on our own initiative, and in our own words.

Related Books, Articles and Films

Mass Incarceration, Criminal Justice, Gang Documentation

- Michelle Alexander, "The New Jim Crow: How the War on Drugs Gave Birth to a Permanent American Undercaste." *The Nation*, March 9, 2010. http://www.thenation.com/article/new-jim-crow/.

- Michelle Alexander, *The New Jim Crow*. This book asserts with extensive documentation that mass incarceration constitutes a new system of racial oppression similar to slavery.

- Angela Davis, "Masked Racism: Reflections on the Prison Industrial Complex." In *Colorlines*, September 10, 1998. In this article, Davis provides a succinct analysis of the evolution of U.S. prisons to being for-profit businesses in themselves that in turn often force inmates to work for other private industries for little or nothing—a modern day slavery.

- *The Atlantic*, *Angola for Life*, a short 14-minute film produced by *The Atlantic* on the topic of prison slavery. http://www.theatlantic.com/business/archive/2015/09/prison-labor-in-america/406177/. The review and summary of the film is found on this link as well.

- Manny Marable, *Racializing Justice, Disenfranchising Lives: The Racism, Criminal Justice, and Law Reader.*

- City of San Diego, "Frequently Asked Questions Regarding Identifying Gangs and Gang Members." https://www.sandiego.gov/sites/default/files/legacy/gangcommission/pdf/sgufaq.pdf.

- *African Elements: Explorations in Black and Africana Studies,* "Guest Lecture: Guilty by Association? Aaron Harvey and Brandon 'Tiny Doo' Duncan Speak at San Diego City College," June 12, 2015. Filmed by Professor Darius Spearman. http://africanelements.org/guest-lecture-guilty-by-association-aaron-harvey-and-brandon-tiny-doo-duncan-speak-at-san-diego-city-college/.

Palestine

- *If Americans Knew,* http://www.ifamericansknew.org/history/. This website provides a brief history of Palestine and the creation of Israel, with links within the site to more detailed information.

- Jimmy Carter, *Peace, Not Apartheid.* In this book, President Jimmy Carter argues that Israeli colonization of Palestine makes a lasting peace impossible.

Drug Addiction and Treatment

- *New York Times* editorial board, "Drug Deaths Reach White America," January 16, 2016. This editorial asserts that a different response to drug addiction is applied when it is recognized that the victims are white. http://www.nytimes.com/2016/01/25/opinion/drug-deaths-reach-white-america.html?_r=0.

- Tim Wise, "White Denial: America's Persistent and Increasingly Dangerous Pastime," November 25, 2015. http://www.timwise.org/2015/11/white-denial-americas-persistent-and-increasingly-dangerous-pastime/. In this article, originally written for CNN, Wise presents a well-documented argument regarding "colorblindness" or the idea that we live in a post-racial society. Wise is also the author of *Between Barack and a Hard Place,* in which he further explains the fallacies of the idea that we live in a post-racial society.

Addictions

- Gabor Maté, "Addictions Originate in Unhappiness—and Compassion Could Be the Cure." *Yes! Magazine*, Summer 2011 issue. This Canadian physician, author of *In the Realm of Hungry Ghosts: Close Encounters With Addiction*, asserts that addiction is not a manifestation of personal weakness but rather a response to childhood suffering and severe life stressors. http://www. yesmagazine.org/issues/beyond-prisons/why-punish-pain.

Childhood Trauma, Neglect

- *American Academy of Experts in Traumatic Stress*. This website provides insights into the psychological effects on the brain due to trauma. This particular link is about the consequences of early childhood trauma. http://www.aaets.org/article196.htm.

Sex Workers

- Sex Workers Project. This group writes: "As the only U.S. organization meeting the needs of both sex workers and trafficking victims, the Sex Workers Project serves a marginalized community that few others reach. We engage in policy and media advocacy, community education and human rights documentation, working to create a world that is safe for sex workers and where human trafficking does not exist." http://sexworkersproject.org/.

Related Topics

- Tavis Smiley, *Covenant With Black America*. Each chapter, written by a different contributor, outlines one key issue and provides a list of resources, suggestions for action, and a checklist for what concerned citizens can do to keep their communities progressing socially, politically, and economically.

- *African Elements: Explorations in Black and Africana Studies*, "Guest Lecture: Elbert 'Big Man' Howard Speaks at San Diego's

Jacobs Center for Neighborhood Innovation" (June 7, 2015), June 15, 2015. Filmed by Professor Darius Spearman. http://africanelements.org/guest-lecture-elbert-big-man-howard-june-7-2015/.

- Darius Spearman on *African Elements: Explorations in Black and Africana Studies*, "The Conservative Era From Reagan to Obama—Introduction," April 7, 2013. http://africanelements.org/episode-14/.

- Barbara Ehrenreich, "It Is Expensive to Be Poor" from the January 13, 2014 edition of *The Atlantic*. http://www.theatlantic.com/business/archive/2014/01/it-is-expensive-to-be-poor/282979/. In addition to documenting how incredibly difficult it is to get ahead if you're poor, Ehrenreich traces the history of blaming the poor for being lazy, shiftless, and irresponsible, and therefore responsible for their own situation.

Gangs

- Patrick Regan, "Causes of Gang Violence Cannot Be Solved by Enforcement Alone." *The Guardian*, October 27, 2012. http://www.theguardian.com/commentisfree/2012/oct/28/causes-gang-violence-complex-enforcement.

- Shane Liddick in *San Diego City Beat*, August, 2004. Part I: "Gangland San Diego: Gang Activity in America's Finest City," http://sdcitybeat.com/article-1888-gang-land-san-diego.html. Part II: "Gangland America: Finding Common Ground Between Street Gangs, Fraternities and Warring Nations," http://sdcitybeat.com/article-1910-GANGLAND-AMERICA.html.

Prison Gangs

- Jeffrey Toobin, "This Is My Jail." *The New Yorker*, April 14, 2014. http://www.newyorker.com/magazine/2014/04/14/this-is-my-jail.

- Graeme Wood, "How Gangs Took Over Prisons." *The Atlantic*, October 2014. http://www.theatlantic.com/magazine/archive/2014/10/how-gangs-took-over-prisons/379330/.

- David Skarbek and Courtney Michaluk, "To End Prison Gangs, It's Time to Break Up the Largest Prisons." *Politico*, May 13, 2015. http://www.politico.com/agenda/story/2015/05/end-prison-gangs-break-largest-prisons-000034.

Immigration

- Nicholas J. Cull and David Carrasco, *Alambrista and the U.S.–Mexico Border: Film, Music, and Stories of Undocumented Immigrants*. 2004.

Journal Questions

- Describe the role of gangs in your community and your life.

- Flaco illustrates his second chances. Write about a meaningful second chance you have had in your life.

- Many of the authors have a turning point in their life. Write about a turning point in your own life.

- Alberto Vasquez discusses how he lacked self-confidence when he went to the university. Write about a time in your life when you did not have self-confidence and how you handled it.

- Explain how your family has influenced your decisions and other aspects of your life.

- Write about the neighborhood you grew up in and how it has affected your life and decisions.

- What are some of the positive and/or negative aspects of the neighborhood where you grew up?

- How would people describe your neighborhood, and would you agree with their descriptions? How does the reality of your neighborhood match or challenge other people's assumptions?

- What experiences have you had with the police, the border patrol or law enforcement in general?

- Have you ever experienced the loss of someone who was close to you? How has that experience impacted your life?

- Have you or someone you know ever been impacted by the criminal justice system?

- How has your race and ethnicity impacted your life?

- How has your appearance affected your life or how people treat you?

- Write about speaking a language other than standard English at home.

- In what ways has immigration impacted your family or community?

- Write about how a border has impacted your life. This could be an international border, an informal or personal border.

- In what ways are you privileged or not privileged?

- Have you or someone you know ever been in a toxic relationship? What lessons can be learned from this experience?

- Write about some of the assumptions people make about you based on your race, religion, sexuality, gender, etc.

- Have you ever made assumptions about a group of people based on an experience that you have had? What are your assumptions about groups of people based on?

- Has math or another subject ever been a barrier to your achieving your goals? Explain. Why do you think this happened to you?

- Write about an educational experience that turned your life around for better or for worse.

- Many of the stories in this book end in change. Describe the aspects of your life that you would like to change or cultivate.

- Many of these stories confront traumatic experiences. Write about how you or anyone you have known has experienced something similar.

- Describe your experience—or that of someone you know—with homelessness. Or, what is your reaction when you walk past a homeless person, or someone begging?

- Have you or has anyone you know dealt with serious mental or physical health challenges? Explain the situation.

- If you could identify one person that you know to read one story in this book, who would it be and which story would it be? Explain the reasons for your choices.

- If you could interview one of the authors, who would you pick? What would you ask and how do you think they would answer?

- Write a dialogue between you and one of the authors, or choose two authors and write a dialogue between them.

- Imagine that you are the 20th author for this anthology. Write your story.

Discussion Questions

- How do these stories illustrate the resilience and strength of the author(s)?

- How have the stories in this book impacted you? How do stories help us learn about the world? Consider the role of stories in education and in influencing our understanding of the world.

- Write a letter to a local lawmaker in which you tell that person your concerns about a situation that comes up in these stories with your recommendations of what needs to be done to improve this situation to give those impacted opportunities to thrive.

- It has been said that those who are in prison are not the only ones who serve time, but the families also serve time. How do these stories illustrate that?

- Based on these stories, what does the criminal justice system currently look like? What should it look like?